ROMANY JUSTICE

6th April 89.

Henry P. Chalk

ROMANY JUSTICE

H. Chalk

ARTHUR H. STOCKWELL LTD.
Elms Court   Ilfracombe
Devon

By the same author:
The Devil Sits Among The Congregation

ISBN 0 7223 2288-7

*Printed in Great Britain by
Arthur H. Stockwell Ltd.
Elms Court   Ilfracombe
Devon*

CONTENTS

ROMANY JUSTICE

SYNOPSIS

This story is about how smuggled contraband was delivered to its recipients across the South of England, in the days before the coming of trains and motor cars. In this case it was done by a family of Romany gypsies who became known as the "Vagabond Riders", travelling the South of England in their wagons after picking up their illicit goods from a gypsy camp on the Dorset Downs.

The head of the family concerned was a man in his late forties, and was known to all who had dealings with him as "Jobey". He really was a rough tough man. He had three sons who were also like their father; hard, headstrong and daring. All were excellent horsemen and good fighters. They mainly made their living as horse dealers. Their names were "Ned" the eldest; "Tosho" came next; with "Owl" the youngest. Their mother, and of course the wife of Jobey, was known to her family and friends as Ma' Marti. She was also known far and wide as one who had a great insight into the future, which no doubt made her a much sought-after fortune-teller.

Read about the intrigue and loves of her family. I hope you enjoy the wild tales of these Romany people.

H.C.

In this story quite a few Romany words are used. You must remember that it is a spoken language, not a written one. Mainly I have used the normal word, then the Romany word which appears in brackets. This may not be strictly adhered to, sometimes the reverse is the case, according to the way the story flows. For example see below:—

Solivardo	—	Light Cart
Petulengro	—	A Farrier, or the name Smith
Rikkeni Chavi	—	Beautiful Girl
Cannie-Moosh	—	Gamekeeper
Drabengro	—	Doctor
Cosh	—	Stick
Shoshi	—	Rabbit
Dunnik	—	Cow
Toovalo	—	To Smoke, or Tobacco
Boro-Divvas	—	Wedding Feast
Chovihani	—	A Witch
Vardo	—	A Living Wagon
Pookerin-Cosh	—	Signpost
Boro-Rye	—	Squire, or Big Man
Moosh	—	A Man
Bouri-Cannie	—	Pheasant
Gorgio	—	House Dweller
Pal	—	Brother
Swegler	—	Pipe
Tompad	—	The Vicar
Boshomengro	—	Fiddler, or Violinist
Chop the Groi	—	Change Horses
Boler	—	Wheel
Dadrus	—	Father
Atching-Tan	—	Camp
Bori-Diklo	—	Headscarf
Kash-Yag	—	Fire
Kavvi-Saster	—	Long Iron Bar
Meski	—	Gypsy Tea
Kitchema	—	Pub
Joskin	—	Estate Worker

The Job

CHAPTER 1

It was a grey November day when Jobey and his youngest son Owl took one of their wagon wheels down to the forge at Tisbury, where the brother of the smith was a wheelright.

Jobey pulled up the four-wheeled gig (solivardo) outside of the blacksmith's forge. He climbed down from his seat and walked in, followed by Owl.

"Well! Well!" exclaimed the blacksmith. " 'Tiz old Jobey. I haven't seen you for ages. How are you?"

"Fairish" replied Jobey.

"And young Owl. Just look at him. My God boy, you do grow. Nearly as big as your dad you are."

"Good grub" replied Jobey.

The blacksmith laughed. "Horse lost a shoe?" he asked.

"No, got trouble with a wheel (boler). Spoke's coming loose — won't go much longer."

"Fetch it in for your dad, Owl," said the smith (petulengro). I'm not busy today. Just making up a pair of shoes for a farmer's horse for next week" he explained.

Owl came back rolling the wheel to lean it against the door.

The smith came over to examine it. "Hum,m,m," he went, "can you come back tomorrow Jobey? You see we shall have to make some parts."

"That's fine, tomorrow will do" he replied.

"Come any time after midday — she'll be ready by then."

Jobey and the smith (petulengro) smacked palms on the deal.

"Is it alright to leave me 'orse?" asked Jobey "I gotta get bread for Ma' Marti."

"Sure 'tiz alright. Just leave her where you like."

The two Romanies wandered off down the street to purchase bread, jam and cheese, which they carried off in a clean sack.

As they wandered back to the forge to collect their solivardo, a rider reined in beside them.

"Hello!" he greeted them. "I believe you are Jobey Doe the travelling man?"

"That's me" replied Jobey. "What's the trouble?"

"No trouble my friend. You see I need a job done and I was wondering if you would do it for me. Money's good. Work's easy. What do you say?"

"I shall need to know more than that!" replied Jobey.

"And so you shall my friend. Can you spare time to have a drink and a chat with me?"

At this juncture the man got off his horse saying "Follow me men."

He led them along to the tavern, where he tied his horse to the hitch-rail, and led the two Romanies into the inn where they all sat down at a table.

"Ale, landlord!" shouted the man.

The landlord brought three jugs of ale.

"Can you bring us bread, cheese and pickled onions?" asked the man.

"My pleasure sir" replied the landlord, as they all took a quaff at the lovely fresh-looking ale.

The man said "I'm Bill Clover, I'm what you might call a go-between man."

The food came now as ordered, and Bill Clover paid the landlord, who promptly went back to dealing with his beer barrels.

"Now Jobey, the job is this," said Bill Clover, dropping his voice to a whisper. "Now I want you, if you will mind, because you are not obliged to accept the job in any way. However, I will explain because I know you can be trusted. I believe you travel between Dorchester and Salisbury horse dealing and working at fairs and the like. Is that true?" he asked.

" 'Tiz true" agreed Jobey. "Horse dealing mainly."

Owl nodded.

"Good! Now in Dorset, at a certain place, I would like you to pick up some goods for me, and bring 'em quietly up to this area. (No one must ever know mind.) Where are you now?" he asked.

"On the common" replied Jobey. "What sort of goods is it?" asked Jobey.

"Well 'tiz collecting neatly packed stuff. It's in five-gallon barrels."

"What's in 'em?" asked Jobey.

"French Brandy! It's the finest men can make, and money can buy."

Owl looked at his father (dadrus), as Bill Clover continued.

"The thing is Jobey, nobody will ever suspect that you are carrying a drop of contraband, now would they? Have you ever been stopped and searched by the troopers or custom's men for that matter?"

"Never!" replied Jobey.

"Then what do 'ee say Jobey me lad?"

"How much?" asked Jobey.

"I will pay you one crown for each barrel that you deliver to me. How's that?" Without waiting for a reply he continued. "Now inside your wagon is a bunk-bed on each side. Now the top lifts up, leaving a storage space below. Is that right?"

"Ah! 'tis true" agreed Jobey.

"Well now, if your beds run the length of the wagon, you can easily put eight barrels in each side. That's sixteen barrels at a crown a piece — that's four guineas a trip for one wagon. Now if you have two wagons, that's eight guineas a trip."

"How many trips have I got to make?" asked Jobey.

"I reckon one a month, and that's roughly when the boat lands the stuff; according to the moon and tide, you understand. Now all you have to do is to be camped near King Henry's Barn. The rest is easy. You see Jobey, between three and four o'clock in the morning, a string of pack-ponies will arrive at your camp carrying the goods. All you have to do is load 'em up into your wagon. Then, as usual, make your way up here, not hurrying, but acting normal. I shall pick 'em up from you, and pay you the cash at that time. How about it Jobey?"

"Can but try I reckon. We'll think about it" he promised.

"Look Jobey, I'm sure you will do it. Now here's a length of blue ribbon. Tie this to your wagon door as you camp at King Henry's Barn. You do know where it is, don't you?"

"Yes I know, it's on the downs just off the Dorchester road."

"You got it Jobey."

The men smacked palms on it, with Jobey saying "I might back out yet mind."

Bill Clover laughed "Not you old son, not you." He stood up now asking "Are you alright for money, Jobey?"

"Yeah, I'm fine" he answered.

Bill Clover drained his glass, then said, "See you again men." He went out now, to gallop away moments later towards Fonthill.

*   *   *

"What do you reckon Pa?" asked Owl.

"Well, as I sees it, what have we got to lose son? If we makes four guineas a trip, that must be fifty guineas a year. In about five years, we could be rich. But then we must see what Ma' Marti says I reckon. She's the one who can tell the future eh?"

Owl grinned, "Yeah I reckon she'll agree somehow. It will be a bit of excitement anyway."

The two men drained their glasses and wandered back to collect their solivardo.

As they drove away from the blacksmith's shop, they noticed that their wheel (boler) had already been knocked to pieces, and the job of repairing it started.

They arrived back at the common, and pulled in under the trees to their camp (atching-tan) which means camping site. Ned was sat by the fire talking to Ma' Marti, and his sister Rikkeni. Rikkeni means beautiful, and chavi means girl. The family called her Rikkeni-Chavi. She really was a beautiful girl. In other words, he was talking to his mother and sister.

"Can't mend it eh?" inquired Ned.

"Tomorrow" replied Jobey. "Where's Tosho?" he asked, almost in the same breath.

"Collecting sticks" replied Ma' Marti.

Everyone settled around the fire now, and very soon Tosho came back carrying a big bundle of sticks, which he dumped by the fire, and promptly sat on them.

"Good trip Pa?"

"Yeah. Now I wants you all here to listen to what I says. When I finished, I wants everybody's opinion on what I says. Do you all understand?"

They all nodded, seeing that Pa' Jobey was serious.

He then related to them all that the man Bill Clover had said — not missing out anything.

The family looked at each other.

Ned spoke first, "I'm with you Pa, you can count on me."

Within minutes, they had all agreed. Ma' Marti wanted to consult her crystal ball. They could see her in her wagon, through the window, with her headscarf (bori-diklo) on, peeping in between her hands, at the ball.

She came out at last, saying "There will be problems. But the general outlook is good. Yes, why not I says!"

There was great excitement in the family now as they all agreed to set out on this new adventure of transporting the contraband from the Dorchester area up to the Salisbury area, where there was obviously a good market.

*   *   *

Next day Pa' Jobey and Owl set off in the solivardo to collect the repaired boler. As they pulled up at the forge they could see the repaired boler outside leaning against the wall. It was painted in its original colour — yellow and red.

Jobey walked in.

"She's done and ready" called the petulengro.

Jobey took out a guinea. "Will that cover?" he asked.

"Yep, and you've got change to come."

"Keep it" replied Jobey, "and thanks. I really wants another living wagon (vardo). Should you know of one, I'd be obliged."

"I do know of one now" replied the smith. "See Jimmy Williams at Long Barn Farm, he makes 'em. He used to travel until he lost a leg. Now he builds living wagons."

"Where's Long Barn Farm?"

"Come with me Jobey." The smith took Jobey to the corner of the green and pointed — "That's it."

"Thanks" replied Jobey. "I'll go see him now."

With the boler loaded into the solivardo, they drove off towards Long Barn Farm.

In the yard they noticed that the doors of the barn were wide open. There was a man painting a very nice looking living wagon (vardo).

"Hello!" shouted Jobey.

The man looked up. "Business is it?" he asked.

"Yeah, I'm looking for a wagon.

The man put his paint on an old table and came towards them.

"The smith sent me" explained Jobey.

"Take a look at 'un," suggested Mr Williams. "Know the smith then?" he asked.

"Always deals with the smith" replied Jobey, as they gave the wagon a good look over.

"Got another out back if this one don't suit" suggested Mr Williams. "It's lighter made than this one, pulls easier. The smith does all my ironwork for me you know."

They followed the wagon builder out to the backyard where the travelling men looked over this much lighter wagon.

"How much?" asked Jobey.

"Fifty guineas" came the reply.

"No, too much."

"Forty-five then."

"Forget it" replied Jobey as he turned to walk away. "I only paid twenty-seven guineas for my big wagon, and that's only three years old."

"Thirty guineas" shouted Mr Williams thinking that Jobey was leaving.

Jobey came back saying "That's more like the price range for Jobey Doe."

The wagon builder looked at Jobey. "You're Jobey Doe?" he asked.

"Ah, that's right, and this is Owl my son."

"Well bugger my old boots" exclaimed Mr Williams. "I'm like a cousin of yours. You see your father's sister, was my wife's mother. I used to travel until I lost my leg when a horse spooked in a thunderstorm. Now I builds vardos. Bought this place you see."

The three men greeted each other, and went to sit on some old chairs in the barn, to chat.

"Yes, he had made a nice workshop out of the old barn."

Before they left to go back to the common, Jobey had bought the light vardo for twenty-five guineas, and would collect it tomorrow — off home now to put the newly repaired boler back on their own vardo.

"I noticed one thing" said Owl when the job was done and the family stood looking at it. "The bolers on this wagon are the same as the ones on the new wagon."

"That's why I picked 'un" replied Pa' Jobey.

Supper was ready now — the main meal of the day. Ma' Marti and Rikkeni were dishing it up.

As they all sat around the fire inside of the canvas wall surround, Pa' suggested that he would drive one vardo, the big one; while Ma' and Rikkeni the new one; Owl would drive the solivardo; Ned and Tosho would ride the loose horses, as forward and rear scouts; while the spare horses could be tied behind the vardos. It was all agreed.

Later that night, as Ma' and Rikkeni went to their vardo to sleep, the men sat and chatted about their new adventure that was about to start. One by one they dozed off. These Romany folk always erected a six-foot high roll of canvas in a good circle, and lit a fire in the middle. The menfolk sat with their back to the canvas and simply slept where they were. They were a wild healthy type of people who knew no other life-style. However, contrary to some folks' belief, they do not go short of food. There is always the rabbit (shoshi) to eat. Shoshi, of course, is the Romany word for rabbit.

Next morning, Ned and Tosho built up the wood fire (kash-yag), while Owl resited the kavvi-saster, which is the long iron bar which is pushed into the ground. It has a hook on one end on which the pot or kettle is hung over the fire. The remains of last night's supper is usually hotted up to form a hot early morning drink of soup.

Ma' Marti came now with Rikkeni, and started to fry eggs and bacon, with fried bread and potatoes — sipping a bowl of hot soup as they worked.

The men went off to gather a large pile of wood for the day's fire.

Now, with lots of gypsy tea (meski) made, they all sat around chatting and enjoying their breakfast. Two meals a day was all these people ever looked forward to, or ever had. They ate morning and evening. They mainly used gypsy tea to drink. That is, the dried leaves of the Creeping Dead Nettle, which can easily be found growing in dampish shady places such as hedgerow bottoms etc. It is also a mild laxative.

After breakfast, Ma' Marti, Rikkeni and Pa' Jobey set off in the solivardo to collect the new wagon, with the horse that would pull it harnessed and tied on behind. They were never in a hurry these Romany folk — they travelled along at a leisurely pace.

At last Tisbury came in sight. Along now to see Jimmy Williams.

After doing some shopping, the two women set out for the common, while Jobey on the return journey called at the King's Arms Tavern (kitchema), which means a pub. He wanted a word with Bill Clover.

The bar was empty when Jobey arrived. A jug of ale was set before him. "Now I've got good news for you" explained Jobey. "I've got two wagons now, and I'm setting out the day after tomorrow."

"Excellent!" replied Bill, "you should be there by next Sunday."

"Yes" agreed Jobey.

"Well, Sunday is a good night for beaching a cargo. Therefore, early on Monday, the pack-ponies should arrive at your camp. If they don't come, stay until they do."

"Got ya" replied Jobey. "And tie that ribbon you gave me on my wagon door."

"Yes, that will do. They know by that who to give the kegs to."

Jobey said "Farewell", and left for the common.

The two women were almost home when Jobey came trotting up in the solivardo.

"She runs well Pa', and the turntable will go right round at any angle. I like it."

"Thought you would" replied Jobey.

Everyone came now to see the new vardo — it did look posh. There was lots to do as they prepared to leave. Madcap would look after their camping site until they returned. This common was set aside for these travelling folk by the owner. But, even so, someone else could come in and take their site.

CHAPTER 2

Early next morning, the family set out for King Henry's Barn, which was a recognized camping site for travelling folk such as Romanies.

Pa' drove the leading vardo, with Ned riding on ahead on his horse Balogee. Ma' Marti and Rikkeni came next with the new vardo, while Owl drove the solivardo behind that, followed in the rear by Tosho on his horse Moonlight.

They travelled along at their normal pace and finally arrived at their destination. After selecting an area to camp on, they pulled in and set up their cooking things.

It was the second night when the pack-ponies came. The moon was setting in the west, and the lads, with Pa' Jobey, were sleeping around the fire, when suddenly from across the downs, walking in twos, and one pair behind the other in a long line, came the pack-ponies. They came straight into the camp, and immediately started to unload their goods.

Jobey went out to see the men. All they told him was, "Just load up your wagon my son, and leave at first light."

The boys soon had the barrels stored away under Jobey's instructions. Breakfast was being cooked and tea (meski), was made. Everyone marvelled at how quickly the pack train had unloaded and disappeared. They were packing up to leave now.

The journey back was quite uneventful. The barrels were delivered to Bill Clover, and the money as agreed, was paid over.

This type of trip was carried out five times — then it happened. It was after the fifth trip; Ned was asked by Bill Clover to deliver two kegs of brandy to the old Manor House. All was arranged. He was to see no one, but to simply put the kegs in the stables where his lordship (boro-rye) kept his horses. Boro-rye means big man, or squire. Ned was told to hide the kegs in the hay in the empty stall at

19

the far end. He was doing this at midnight as per his instructions. As he came out of the stables after hiding the last keg, he was suddenly faced by a man with a musket, who stood there in the moonlight.

"Got you matey" he bellowed. And "Who might you be?"

"What's it to you?" asked Ned.

"I'm in charge here because his lordship has been called away urgent like, and he's left me in charge. That's what it is to me. Now who are you?"

Ned did not reply. His first reaction was to leap on his horse and run for it. He couldn't do that because the musket was aimed at him. 'I wonder if it's loaded?' he thought.

"So you got no answer to my question" then snarled the man. "Of course I'm within my rights if I shot you. However I shall have the pleasure of being thanked by his lordship when he returns in two days' time. Now it's the lock-up for you matey." He motioned for Ned to walk in front of him, goading him on with the barrel of his musket.

Ned went along with it thinking that all would be well when the squire (boro-rye) came back, and Bill Clover got to know about it. He would soon put it right.

He was being pushed along now rather roughly towards the west side of the Manor House. The man opened the door, covering Ned with the musket as he did so. Inside now, along a stone passage that was lit by an oil-lamp which stood in a wall bracket. The man took the lamp as they passed. At the end of the passage, Ned was told to turn right down some stairs into a huge cellar where all different types of barrels were stored. "Stand still," he was told. The man opened a door in the wall which squeaked on its old hinges. Fresh air struck at Ned as he was goaded inside. As the lamplight flickered, he noticed a raised wooden bench in the corner of a stone-built room. It was about ten-foot square. "You won't get out of there matey" he said boastfully. The door was slammed and the key was turned in the lock.

Ned felt awful. He had never ever been shut up in a house before; not ever. He felt like crying; but however, he would get out somehow. He could feel the cool night air coming in from a small barred window which was about eighteen inches square. It seemed to reassure him. As his eyes grew used to the dim light, he could see that the window looked out through a tunnel.

'I know where I am now' he thought. 'This is the east side of the house. Now years ago my grandfather told me that they used to drive cattle into these cellars from out in the park there. Yes, he said the entrance was through a tunnel under the east terrace. They put the cattle in here to stop marauding tribes from stealing them; but in more recent times the cellars had been altered.'

He shook at the bars. But they were solid and about one inch thick. So he sat on his bench to think it over. He knew his horse would go home on its own. It was probably back at the campsite right now. He started to doze off a bit now. Something would happen tomorrow.

*   *   *

Yes, his horse did run away, and was very soon racing through the night back to the common where it came and pushed at the canvas surround with its nose.

"Is that you Ned?" asked Owl. No reply. "Ned!" he called. So Owl got up and went to see, followed closely by Tosho. But no Ned, only Balogee standing there head drooping.

The two lads took care of Ned's horse, after which they woke Pa' Jobey, telling him that the horse had returned but no Ned.

The first thing that Pa' Jobey said was "Somebody caught him I reckon. He would never fall off a horse that's for sure." He sat there just thinking for a while. "Right boys, here's my plan. Get some sleep, then we'll go find him tomorrow at first light."

"Yeah," agreed Owl, "we can start at the King's Arms by asking Bill Clover if he knows anything."

"We'll do that son, now get some rest he might have come back by daylight, after all, he can fight any man."

The lads went back to their places by the fire. But they did not sleep. Owl wanted to go and find him right there and then, but Tosho said "Where do we start?"

Dawn broke at last. The lads had the three horses ready. After a hot drink and some bread and cheese, they set out to find Ned. First they went to the King's Arms. They had to knock up Bill Clover.

"What's up?" he demanded angrily from the bedroom window.

" 'Tis me Jobey!"

"Oh, I'm coming down then" replied Bill.

Within minutes, Bill the landlord stood on the doorstep. Jobey explained why he was there.

"Damn funny!" replied Big Bill. "Look men, come in and sit down while I ride up to the Manor to see if I can find out anything there."

He quickly dressed, and went riding off on one of the men's horses, not bothering to waste time harnessing his own.

He came up to the Manor and knocked on the west door. It was soon opened by the 'butler chap' who simply said "Yes sir?"

"May I speak with his lordship?" asked Bill.

"Sorry sir, his lordship has been called away urgently. He will of course be back in a day or so. Can your business wait sir?"

"Not really" replied Bill. "I have come about the loss of a neighbour's son. We believe he came this way last night and got himself lost. He's a stranger to this area you see."

"Well" replied the man, "we do have a man in the cellar cell, but we shall keep him until his lordship returns. He must decide what's to be done with him."

"He might well be the man I'm here about" replied Bill. "May I see him?"

"Well sir, I could let you peep through the spyhole, but that is all."

"Very good I shall be satisfied with that."

"This way sir."

Portly Bill Clover followed the butler along the passage and down to the cellar where the butler motioned to Bill to peep through the spyhole — which he did. Sure enough there was Ned.

As they walked away, Bill asked, "How did you catch him then?"

"Well, it was easy sir, I just took a stroll around at midnight before going to bed. My boss being away you see, and there he was coming out of the stables. 'He's up to no good' I thought. I fortunately had a musket, so at gunpoint I brought him in here. The master will be pleased with me when he gets back, you'll see. I'm sure to get a pat on the back."

Bill thanked the man, mounted his horse and rode off. Back at the King's Arms, he reined in from a good gallop, slipped from his horse, and went quickly indoors to the waiting men.

"Any luck?" asked Jobey.

"Yes, I found him."

"Is he alright?"

"Yes, he's fine. Now sit down lads, I have worked out a plan on my way home to free him. Ned is unharmed, but first let me get some hot tea from the kitchen."

Bill's wife was up now. "Who are those men in the other room?" she asked.

"Friends" he replied, "they have a spot of trouble and I can help. Right now I need some tea, dear."

"Very well, I can bring it through in just a minute. Ham and new bread as well, if you like?"

"Now that's what I calls right 'andsome, me dear. I'll leave it to you then."

Bill went back to the men. "Right, now gather round and listen to my plan. First I must tell you that Ned is in the cellar, in like a prison cell. He was taken there at the point of a musket by the butler. That must have been when his horse ran away and went back to you. Now first having explained where he is, I must now tell you that the butler chap who put him there was having a walk round at midnight when he saw Ned about to leave the stables. That was when he held him up with the musket and put him in the cell as a prisoner. He thinks his lordship, who was called away suddenly, will praise him up when he gets back, for catching Ned. I dare not tell him anything of course, but he is quite wrong there. Now men, here's my plan. First I need to get hold of a man called "Madcap Jimmy King". Now is the King family camped up there near you on the common?"

"Yes, he's there all right" replied Owl.

"Right, here's my plan, listen carefully. This is what I want you to do. Now you Owl, you being the smallest; can you be here at midnight tonight riding your horse and leading Ned's? He will need his to ride home on you see."

"You sound certain" remarked Jobey.

"You bet I am, but you must leave it to me. Trust me Jobey."

The tea, ham, bread and pickles arrived now. The men soon demolished it.

"Now chaps, never again must one man go out alone. He must be accompanied or shadowed by somebody else, then this sort of thing can't happen."

Jobey and the two brothers agreed.

"Now you chaps go home, and by this time tomorrow we shall have a happy outcome to this situation, you'll see. Now you must trust me Jobey."

"I can trust you Bill Clover" replied Jobey, "and thank you. But if you need help, call on we three. We can bring twenty men if needs be. Don't forget that mind."

The men went home now, while Bill Clover had a wash and shave. He set out now for the common to first of all find Madcap Jimmy King. He was called Madcap because he always wore a velvet cap with a button on top, but he always had the peak taken off, so that it fitted like a skull-cap, or as he said 'a small bucket'. He was also known for doing the most daring things imaginable. Yes he was a real hell-raiser. Therefore as Bill Clover had rightly thought 'he was just the man for the job he had in mind'. (It proved so right, as you will see.)

As he pulled up by the gate, that led onto the common, several men came from the bushes and stood behind the gate.

One old fellow said "What do 'ee want mister?"

"I wants to see Madcap Jimmy King" replied Bill.

"Nobody 'ere by that name" he replied. "No. No." They all murmured in agreement.

"Well" replied Bill, "it's a matter of life or death for one of your people. Only Madcap can save this man."

At that moment, Owl came running, followed by Madcap, who leapt over the five barred gate, grinning like a Cheshire cat with his cap pulled well down.

He stood there in the road saying "What's the trouble landlord?"

Bill got down off his horse. "Look Madcap, I badly need your help old son." Then lowering his voice he told him about Ned being held prisoner, and of the way that only he, Madcap Jimmy, could help.

Owl was amazed as he listened. "You can do it" said Owl encouragingly, "because I shall be with you."

"Consider it done then landlord," replied Madcap, with his mighty grin.

They slapped palms on it, and arranged to be at Bill's disposal by eleven-thirty that night at the King's Arms.

"Mind you bring Ned's horse, Owl," called Bill Clover as he mounted up and rode away at a fast trot towards Tisbury.

Bill went straight to the forge where he reined in. Dismounting, he walked in just as the smith was putting a horseshoe back in the fire to reheat it.

"Morning smith" he greeted him.

"Good-day to 'ee landlord," replied the smith. "And what might be the purpose of your visit sir?"

"I need a quiet word in your ear," replied Bill. " 'Tiz worth a guinea mind."

"In that case I'm all ears then," replied the smith, laughing.

Bill went closer to whisper his problem.

"Just a minute" replied the smith, "I've still got the old one."

The smith went into the back stable-like room, only to come back with a large key. "The loop-handle came off, so his lordship brought it down to me to make a new key, leaving this as a pattern."

Big Bill Clover looked at the key. "Now" he asked, can you put an end on this old one, say like a cross T-piece, so that I could use it?"

"Sure I can, and do it while you wait."

"Good job I remembered you making the new one when I had my horse shod last month."

"Ah 'tiz" agreed the smith, "and it's a darned good job I kept the old one."

The smith set to work and soon had a cross T-handle fixed securely on the old key.

Bill kept his word and gave the smith a guinea. "Say not a word mind" he cautioned.

The smith laughed and said "Your secret is safe with me landlord."

Off went Bill now to await nightfall.

*   *   *

It was a Sunday night, and there were hardly any customers at the inn, which was usual for a Sunday in those days. While back at the Manor, Ned was offered a meal by his captors. This is how it went:—

The butler came with a serving wench, who was carrying a dish which contained a meal. The butler unlocked the door, and stood there with his musket trained on Ned.

"Right mister" he snarled, "here is some 'vitals' for 'ee. Now eat it my beauty."

The girl came in, placing the dish in front of Ned on the small rickety table.

Ned was amazed when he looked at the girl. "What you doing here?" he whispered.

"It's all right Ned," she whispered back, "I will help you later, please eat this."

"Stand back by the wall wench," shouted the butler, so as I can keep my eye on matey there."

Ned ate the veg and rabbit portions, and sat back on his rickety chair.

"Think yourself lucky matey" said the butler, "because first thing tomorrow the sweep's boy will be working on cook's chimneys. That's why you got it now. You won't be so lucky tomorrow."

The girl picked up the empty dish, winked at Ned, then walked out. The door was swung shut, and the key turned in the lock.

Ned sat back on his wooden form. It didn't worry him being like this, but he would like his freedom. 'I wonder what she's doing here?' he thought. 'Clare, the daughter of Mr Williams the wagon builder. I know his wife died, then a few years later his daughter disappeared, and here she is all the time, I reckon there is something fishy going on here.' With his warm meal inside him, he lay back on his bench to wait. He started to doze off now.

*   *   *

At eleven-thirty sharp, Owl and Madcap rode up to the rear of the King's Arms. They were about to tap on the door, when Bill Clover came out.

"Right men, have you got everything?" he asked.

"All ready" replied Owl.

"Good, I'll get me horse, then you follow me as quietly as possible."

Off they went, taking it easy, so that the horses made as little noise as possible. At last they came to the park at the top end of which was the big Manor House. As they neared the top end of the park, Bill reined in under some trees. Dismounting, he tied his horse to a low branch. The other two followed suit.

"Gather round men, while I run through the plan to make sure you understand the job in hand. Now just in front of us is a seven-foot high wall. It runs along to the terrace on the east side of the Manor House. Now it's under that terrace, and beneath the house, where Ned is held in a prison cell. I can well remember my father telling me that in this end of the wall is a stone slab. It's about eighteen-inches high, by one-foot two-inches wide. There is an inscription on it which says *In memeory of Bob, a faithful old dog.* Now that stone will lift out. I've brought along a small axe to do that job with. Now once it's lifted out, it will reveal a secret passage which runs behind the wall, and of course under the raised lawn, which of course the wall holds up. Now the passage comes out under the sliding ramp where the beer barrels are slid down into the cellar by the draymen. You see when they raised the land up level to make the croquet lawn years ago, they had to build the wall to hold it up neatly. This was the time when they built the tunnel. My dad saw it on some old plans years ago. 'The tunnel was built for the priests to escape from Cromwell' he reckoned. Nearly all these big old houses have got one somewhere. Anyway, I've got a dark lantern here, and a key to the cell where Ned is being held. Don't ask me to explain how I got it, it will take too long. Now I want you lads to do this job because I'm too bloody fat to do it."

They all giggled at this remark.

Bill squinted at his watch. "I reckon we could make a start now lads. Are you all clear on the job?"

They both agreed.

"When you get to the cellar, there could be things to fall over, but the dark lantern will show them up for you. Ned's cell is the first door on the left as you go in, and don't forget I must have the key back — it's only borrowed, so lock the door behind Ned, and get back here as soon as possible. Let's go men, if you are sure on what to do?"

"Yeah, we're sure, come on," said Madcap impatiently, "I'm dying to get into that place."

Taking their tools, they walked over to the wall. Feeling along, they found the stone with the inscription on it, and set to work at once using the axe as a lever. It worked well, and they soon had the stone out, which revealed a nice-sized passage about three-foot high, by two-foot wide. Madcap crawled in grinning like an ape. The dark lantern was handed in to him and he set about lighting it. At last it was alight. Making sure he had the key, he set off on the eighty-yard crawl to get into the cellar of the Manor House. Owl went in after him, and was soon on his way crawling behind Madcap. Bill flattened himself against the wall listening intently, and saying a silent prayer for success in this venture.

* * *

Meanwhile, Clare the servant girl, was creeping about the house trying to find the key to the cell where Ned was held. She couldn't find it anywhere. Maybe he left it in the cell door, so she made her way along to the cellar. As she felt her way nervously along to the cell, she heard a noise. Just to be on the safe side, she hid behind a pile of barrels. The noise came again; then a flicker of light; soon a man emerged from the brewer's unloading entrance. She was terrified, but she kept still hardly daring to breathe. Now another figure came. They crept past her hiding-place towards Ned's cell. Soon she heard a key turn in the rusty lock.

"You there Ned?" came a whisper.

"Yes. Is that you Owl?"

"Yeah, me and Madcap."

Clare's heart leapt for joy. They had come to rescue Nedder. Soon in the flicker of light she saw Ned and heard the lock being closed again. As the three men passed her she said "Ned, it's me, Clare! Are you alright?"

"Clare!" he exclaimed turning. "What are you doing here?"

"I'm like a prisoner as well," she replied. "If I don't stay here and work the butler is going to give information to the magistrates to have my dad sent to Australia. He said he'd get penal servitude for life if he told the magistrates what my father did; and if I wanted my dad to stay free I was to work here for nothing all my life."

The three men had crowded round her now.

"What did he do, Ned?" she asked in tears now.

"Nothing at all" he replied. "You come with us. Come on right now."

One by one they crawled into the tunnel entrance which was hidden under the brewer's barrel sliding ramp, and made their way slowly back to the entrance at the far end of the croquet lawn.

Owl emerged first, followed by Madcap, Clare, and Ned.

Old Bill Clover was over the moon with joy. "Well done men" he said. "Well done indeed. But who's this little gal you've brought out?"

"This is Clare Williams, daughter of the man who builds the vardos. She's been kept there against her will — it's a long story but it's finished now — I'll explain later."

Ned had a long time to think in his cell, now he had an idea. "Look" he said. "I forgot something, can you come with me Owl? You chaps stay here, we won't be more than fifteen minutes."

"Be careful, Ned," whispered Clare.

He took the small axe and the dark lantern, and disappeared back up the tunnel, followed by Owl. They were soon back in the cellar. Up the steps they went, along the passage, and into the Great Hall. Ned knew something that the others didn't. Over to the big fireplace they crept. It was about two o'clock in the morning. They heard the old stable clock chime the hour. Ned proceeded to feel around the fireplace. Yes it was almost cold. He levered open the big heavy iron fireback of the chimney-breast, just above the huge fire-box. It swung open like an oven door, revealing a large hole. He put his hand in, moving some loose bricks. Yes, it was there, just as he had heard his old grandad once say, 'In these old houses the valuables were kept behind the large iron firebacks, because the fires were never left to go out.' That was how they protected their valuables. But now the fires had been allowed to go out for the sweep's boy to go up the chimney first thing in the morning. Ned filled his coat pockets until they bulged, giving some to Owl.

"Just a little something" he whispered, "to compensate for Clare being held prisoner for nearly three years, and for me of course."

Empty at last, he closed the huge fireback. The men left the house the same way as they had entered, down the long secret passage. They emerged into the fresh air now, to the delight of Clare and the others. The stone was put back in its place. So they mounted up and rode away, with Clare hanging on for dear life behind Ned.

'It's a good job' thought Ned, 'that I heard him say that the fires were being left to go out, so that the sweep's boy could climb the chimney in the morning. Also that the Lord of the Manor (the boro-rye) was due to return that day as well.'

They were riding hell for leather through the night back to the ale house — The King's Arms Tavern.

At the inn, the men dismounted and hitched their mounts to the rail in the backyard. Inside at last, where the landlady had hot tea, and a cold ham and pickle supper ready for them. However, she didn't reckon on seeing a young lady with them, but she was soon catered for.

They all sat around the kitchen table to eat their supper. Many questions were asked. 'How did Ned get put in the cell?' 'How did Clare get shut up to work and slave as she did?' . . . and so on.

After about two hours, with all their questions asked, and answered, Madcap said how much he had enjoyed the evening, and that he should really go now to get his beauty sleep. "Anytime you need a hand landlord, just holler for me. I'll come a-running, and willingly at that." Off he went now, promising to tell Pa' Jobey that Ned was free.

Dawn was coming up now, and Bill Clover promised to tell Ned and family what happened when the squire returned later that day.

"First we must take Clare home to her father" — Dadrus — which is the Romany word for father.

Off went Owl and Ned down to Long Barn, where Mr Williams the vardo builder lived, now that he had a wooden leg.

As they galloped into the yard, the old fellow came out to feed his few hens that seemed to roam everywhere. He looked up at the riders as Ned helped Clare down from his horse.

His mouth dropped open in astonishment, then he shouted "What the hell you doing with my daughter Edward Doe?"

The two brothers laughed as Clare ran up to her father throwing herself into his arms.

"I'll see you in hell for this, stealing her like you have," he shouted.

"Father, it's alright, Ned rescued me, he didn't hurt me. I was like a prisoner. Let me tell you all about it. Where's your vardo?"

"Got no vardo, girl. I'm a house dweller (gorgio) now, I lives in the house here."

"You're a house dweller now then dadrus."

They went indoors now, happy at last, together, while Ned and Owl rode hell for leather back to the common, full of joy at the outcome of the night's work. They had their horses taken from them by Tosho.

"I've had my food" he explained, "leave the nags to me."

The lads were greeted heartily by their parents and Rikkeni.

"Did you get hurt Ned?" asked Ma' Marti.

"No not even a scratch. When I was caught, I just said nothing. You see this butler man (moosh) had a musket, so I just did what he said. I knew Bill Clover would sort it all out when the old boro-rye came back. I also knew that Balogee would come back here — which he did — a good old horse is Balogee. Then when the 'butler moosh' brought me a meal, and Clare brought it in, I was very surprised; after all she had been lost for about three years.''

"How did she come to be there at the Manor House?" asked Rikkeni.

"Well," continued Ned. "She told me that she went there selling clothes-pegs and flowers. This 'butler moosh' answered the door. Now, she not suspecting anything, told him that she would be coming round now like her mother always did, saying of course that her mother had died, and because her father was a man who only had one leg. Whereupon this 'butler moosh' seemed to gloat saying 'I know your father. Now if I cared to open my mouth about something he has done, he would get penal servitude for life, and that's torture for a man with a wooden leg.'

'What's he done then?' she asked. 'He wouldn't want you to know' he replied. 'It was terrible. Now if you don't want him sent away for good, you had better do as you are told my girl.' 'What do you mean?' she asked. 'Well just give me your basket and get in there to work, otherwise I shall go to the magistrates and tell all I know about your father.' She wanted to run away, but as you know she really loved her old father (dadrus). Yes, she really believed this 'butler moosh'. And so it was he made her work in the big kitchens, because she didn't want her father hurt. That butler is a wicked moosh, and no mistake. If I ever meet him again he's for the high jump I can tell you. But we shall see what we shall see, eh Owl? Nobody would work at the Manor you see because of this 'butler moosh', so he had to make somebody work, and he did it with her as a slave.''

"What did her father do?" asked Rikkeni.

"He could do nothing. She had just vanished into thin air. He tried everything that was possible.''

"Oh! what a horrible man that butler is" she exclaimed. "Where is she now?''

"Me and Owl took her back to her dadrus. You see Madcap and Owl got into the cellar through the secret passage. They came along to my cell and called 'Ned are you there?' I answered of course, and I could tell who they were. Now about this time, Clare was creeping about the house trying to find this 'butler moosh's' key to my cell. Hearing voices when she was in the cellar, she hid. They had a dark lantern and she could tell they were there to rescue me. Then as we were leaving the cellar she spoke to me and quickly told me her story. So I said come on you are coming out with us. And she did.

We've just dropped her off at her father's vardo shop. We had to laugh; her father blamed us for taking her away, so we just rode off laughing at him.''

Everyone was happy now, crowding round Ned and Owl as they ate their breakfast, and told their story.

The rest of this episode unfolds back at the old Manor House. Early next morning, at about four-fifteen, the sweep arrived with his cart. His climbing boy was set to work first in the kitchen, where cook was waiting patiently to start her day's work.

The climbing boy was soon up the chimney and working well.

The butler came. "Where's the wench?" he asked.

"Haven't seen her yet" replied cook.

"Send her to me the minute she arrives" he replied rather loudly.

Soon the chimney was swept, and cook was busy at last.

Next came the turn of the lounge chimney, the morning room, and so on. Finally came the turn of the chimney in the Great Hall. There sat at a table and watching like a hawk was the old squire's housekeeper. She was an old family retainer and did not work regular hours. Her job at this moment was to watch and see if the sweep's boy or the sweep touched the security oven behind the fireback, now that it was quite cold of course. Little did they know that it was empty.

As the sweep was packing up to leave, who should come home at that moment in his carriage, none other than the old squire himself. The butler met him at the door and assured him that all was well — pouring him and his lady a drink. When they had changed and rested they came to cook for a meal. During the meal, the butler who of course was serving at table, told the squire that he had captured a man who was prowling around the stables at midnight.

"And what did he say?" asked the squire.

"He simply asked me who I was. So I locked him up in the cellar, and there he is awaiting your pleaasure. I didn't know if you wanted me to fetch the constables or not."

"Is he a big built man?" asked the squire.

"No sir, he is none the less well built."

"Excuse me my dear," said the squire to his wife, "but I really must go and see this prisoner. Lead the way my good man."

The butler proudly led the way down to the old cell in the cellar. He placed the key in the lock, turned it, opened the door and shouted. "Stand up for his lordship the squire."

Squire went in and looked everywhere, then back at the butler who just stood there gaping. The cell was empty.

"Well! Where is he man?" yelled the squire, who was himself an old army officer.

"But! But! He was locked in here, and I have carried the key ever since. Now he's gone. I, I, don't understand. The window bars have not been touched."

Yes, the door was locked, but the prisoner was gone.

"What damn silly game are you playing at man" roared the now very agitated squire, who hated being made a fool of.

"But sire he was locked in here."

"You have been at my damn brandy, blast you, that's what. Now get out of my sight before I lock you up."

His lordship the squire made his way back to his lady in a furious temper. Yes, he was really cross now; while the completely baffled butler set about his work feeling very humbled indeed. Instead of a pat on the back, he now had a kick in the pants.

A little later that day, her ladyship wanted to return some of her valuables back to the safety box behind the Great Hall fireback before it was rekindled. She came with her old housekeeper, a very trusted servant indeed, for the butler to open the safety box. This he did. The housekeeper put her gloved hand into the box to retrieve the necklace case for her ladyship, but the safety box was completely empty. His lordship was called from his study.

When the problem was explained to him, he flew into a furious rage shouting, "It's that damn butler again. That's who it is. I should have known better than to leave him in charge. First he's got a prisoner who isn't even here. Now he's pinched me bloody valuables. Where is he? He's sacked! I'll flay the bounder alive, that's what I'll do."

Now the butler, who was standing by his pantry door just outside of the Great Hall, heard all that was said. He waited not a moment longer. He could stand no more. So he ran upstairs and hurriedly packed his bags, then ran from the house, while the very enraged squire searched high and low for him.

At last he saw his stableman, "Have you seen the butler?" he bellowed.

"Yes sir, he's gone off down the road there hurrying along with a portmanteau."

"Right, now listen to me. Ride like blazes for the constables and tell them that I want that man arrested. He's stolen me valuables from the safety box. In the meantime should he return, I'll damn well shoot the bounder. Go on man, ride like hell."

The stableman was soon going at a full gallop for the constables at Shaftsbury. 'My God' he thought, 'the squire is really mad today. I've never seen him like that before.'

He arrived at the constables' station, and delivered his message from the squire, who was also in those days, a magistrate. This of course had a great influence on these constables. He also described the man to be apprehended. They set out at once, while the stableman trotted back home with his job done.

Later that evening, with the squire calmed down, Big Bill Clover came along to see him. He was shown into the squire's study. After a while he came along to see who the man was that wanted a word with him.

"Hello! there landlord old chap. Is everything alright?"

"Yes sir, all is well."

"Oh yes, I found me brandy. Jolly good show what!"

"And how did your trip go sir?"

"Oh very well old chap. But while I was away me damned butler let me down — acted like a lunatic. He's gone now. Pinched a lot of me valuables ya know. Anyway he's in stir now as they say. Look old chap, can you get me some more brandy next month?"

"How many would you like sir?"

"Well, could do with four, if you could spare that much. Got a friend ya see."

"Yes of course, four it shall be."

After a chat, and a glass of brandy, Bill Clover set off back to his ale house.

When Bill Clover told Jobey about all that had happened at the Manor House he simply said, "I reckon my wife put a curse on that old butler for holding Ned. She is a witch you know."

A witch in the Romany language is a chovihani.

CHAPTER 3

The brandy runs were going well, and the horse dealing which was the family business, seemed to be improving also. Rikkeni was doing well with her leather craft. Yes, all seemed to be running along nicely.

It was a frosty morning; Tosho ate his breakfast, with the family complaining about Madcap. They could hear him chopping wood for his mother, and singing at the same time. He really was making an awful din.

"Who told you that you could sing" shouted Ned.

No response.

He was still chopping when breakfast was finished, so Tosho thought that he would go and tell him to shut up.

As he came up to Madcap he stopped chopping and said "Just the moosh I've been looking for."

"How long have you been looking for me then?" asked Tosho.

"Ages" he replied. "Didn't you hear me calling? Now sit down on that pile of wood and listen to me. I was down in the spinney there that joins this wood to the big wood of the squires, down there," he said, pointing. "There I was collecting wood for Ma' you see, when suddenly I stopped dead in me tracks. There in front of me, no more than four foot away was a mantrap. It had been covered with leaves, but the wind had blown them away. If it hadn't, I would have stepped in it for certain. Now I've got a brainwave. You see I got to thinking that if one of the kids ran off playing down there, it could chop their legs off, and what about one of our lurchers? Kill 'em for sure. Now I reckon it's that keeper. I've seen him watching up here with a spyglass. He don't like us sort, that I know. Now if he thinks he can catch one of us, he's dead wrong, Tosho my old son. Now here's my brainwave. Why don't you and I go down there and move the trap down near his big wood? After all the old

34

boro-rye gave us the rights of this place for as long as we want it, providing we don't touch his pheasants. Well, we don't do we Tosho?''

"Oh no,'' he replied. "Well not much, anyway.''

"Now being as keeper got no rights up here. What do 'ee say my Tosho? Shall we move the trap off our patch so as not to get a little child caught in it, or do we leave it?''

Tosho looked at Madcap, who was grinning now more than usual, then he suggested "We could move it further back down that path, then maybe we might catch a gamekeeper'' he quipped.

Those two lads just fell about laughing. At last they slapped palms on it in agreement, and set off down to where the trap was set. It really was an evil contraption. They pressed a large piece of wood on the trap's tongue. It went off, snapping the wood in half.

"Damn that keeper'' (cannie-moosh), exclaimed Tosho.

They carried the trap almost down to the big wood, where they reset the evil thing in a bed of leaves, covering it up nicely.

"Let the evil old bugger have some of his own medicine,'' suggested Madcap. "It will smarten up the legs of his breeches, I'll be bound.''

After this, they made their way back to the common, telling no one of the prank they had played on the keeper (cannie-moosh).

* * *

It was the next day, about eleven o'clock, when Ma' Marti who was polishing the brasses on her vardo, felt sure she could hear someone calling for help. It came plainly now — "Help!'' She left the vardo to find one of her sons or Jobey. They were all sitting round the fire drinking tea (meski). "There is someone in trouble'' she said. "Can't you hear the cries for help?'' They listened! It came quite clearly now — "Help! Help!''

"Can't hear a thing'' replied Tosho, grinning.

The cries came still louder.

"Better see what 'tiz I reckon'' suggested Pa' Jobey.

So the men went off in the direction of the voice calling for help. It seemed very urgent. Someone was crying out and calling loudly now. Down the path hurried the men. They were well out of bounds from the area allocated to them by the squire. At last they found out what it was. There, lying on the ground, with his legs caught in a huge trap was the gamekeeper (cannie-moosh).

"Get me out for God's sake'' he begged.

Jobey and Ned started to prise the trap jaws open. With more help from Owl they managed it. Keeper rolled himself free but he couldn't stand up — not even with help — he just could not stand.

"I reckon you must see a doctor" (drabengro), suggested Jobey.
"Right, Owl, Ned, get the solibardo."

They ran off at their father's bidding. As they ran Owl said to
Ned, "Fancy getting caught in his own bloody trap, moosh."

"He's hurt real bad" replied Ned.

"Yeah," agreed Tosho. "But who did he set the trap for then?
Answer me that."

Ned didn't speak.

But Owl suggested "To catch one of us, that's what."

"Yeah, I suppose it was" replied Ned. "In which case, it served
the old devil right."

Back they came with the solivardo. They all helped to lift the
gamekeeper into the bed of the cart. Pa' Jobey took the reins and
set off at once for the doctor's house in Tisbury.

As they arrived, Ned jumped down from the cart and banged on
the door; a woman answered his knock.

"Got a man with bad injuries to his legs, ma'am. Can we see the
doctor?"

"Bring him in, I'll fetch him. He is just about to start out on his
rounds."

While the nurse lady ran out through the back to stop the doctor
from riding off, the men carried in the gamekeeper and laid him on
a sofa with his legs up.

The doctor came back now. Seeing the men, he asked, "What's
the trouble here then?"

"Found him with his legs in a mantrap" replied Jobey.

The doctor put a monocle in his eye and started to examine the
damaged legs. After a while, with the keeper howling in pain, he
said, "Leave him here with me, one leg is fractured. I will attend to
him now. You men may go."

The men trooped out and climbed aboard the solivardo.

"I reckon we should go and tell the squire (boro-rye) right now
and hand in his gun. I don't reckon he'll need a gun for a week or
two" remarked Jobey.

Off they went now to drive round to the back door of the Manor
House. Jobey knocked on the door and waited. It was opened
eventually by the old housekeeper.

"Yes?" she asked.

"I need to see the squire" replied Jobey. "His gamekeeper has
been badly hurt."

"Oh! I see. You had better come this way" she invited.

Jobey followed the old housekeeper along a passage, at the end
of which she said "Wait here please." She knocked on a door and

went in closing it behind her. Out she came quite quickly saying "This way please."

Jobey went in. There sat the old squire behind his desk.

"Why, it's you, Jobey! What seems to be the trouble?"

"Well sir, we heard someone calling for help — real bad like — and it seemed to come from the big wood direction; so we ran down the footpath in the spinney, and there lying on the ground was one of your keepers with his feet in a mantrap. Well we struggled and got him out. Fetched our gig, and took him to the doctor. He couldn't stand you see. Now the doctor says he's got a broken leg."

"Do you know who set the trap Jobey?"

"He must have I reckon" replied Jobey. "Nobody else would do such a thing. And who else would own such an evil tool? But I tell you now squire, and I mean it, it's a good job for him that he didn't catch one of our little children in it. You know that, don't you?"

"Yes Jobey, I do realize what you are saying. It seems to me that his evil intentions came back on himself."

"Exactly sir, he forgot where he set it. Well, that's all I came to tell you sir. Oh yes, I got his gun with me outside like."

"Right Jobey, I'll come and fetch it."

"It's still primed, I reckon," continued Jobey.

The squire came out with Jobey and took the gun. He thanked the men for helping so willingly.

"Well, 'twas your gamekeeper, sir. We done it because we knew you would have expected us to."

Jobey took the reins again and drove away.

Back at camp, Madcap came now to see what all the fuss had been about. When he was told he went into fits of laughter.

"Serves him right" he said. "Got some of his own medicine didn't he? I watched him with his spyglass, watching us for days he was. He never did like us, thinks we takes his pheasants (bouricannie), poor old gamekeeper (cannie-moosh). But still squire can get a new one eh?"

Once again he went into one of his Madcap laughs. This time they all joined in.

*　　*　　*

But the squire was furious, he sat and thought about what Jobey had said — 'That he might have caught a young child in it' — 'My God, I can't bear to think of it. A little Romany girl innocently playing there only to have her legs chopped off by a damned evil thing like that. He knows I won't allow it.'

He sent orders to his groom to harness his horse and have it by the back door soonest. As soon as it was ready, he set out for the South Lodge to find his head keeper. He had just come back from his keepering rounds, and was feeding his ferrets.

His lordship reined in and called "Thompson! A word in your ear my man."

Thompson, the head keeper, came over to him at once.

"What's the trouble sir?" he asked.

"There's trouble aplenty" replied the squire. "Now Mr Thompson, I want these orders obeyed at once. Your under keeper has set a mantrap, and the damned fool has walked into it himself. At this moment in time he is at the doctor's house with at least one broken leg. I want that trap collected and taken to the forge to be destroyed — and you will watch the smith do it — when it is done report back to me."

"Yes sir, at once. But where is this trap?"

"It's in the connecting spinney that runs from the common down to the big wood. The Romanies heard him calling for help, so they went to see what the trouble was. He's only got them to thank for saving his life, otherwise he would have bled to death you see. I'm off to see the doctor as soon as possible. You do as I say, then report back to me. I will not have a mantrap anywhere on this estate. Never. And from now on you will be held responsible."

"Yes sir. I wonder where that trap came from?" muttered the keeper.

The squire rode off now to Tisbury. Dismounting, he knocked on the doctor's door. The lady assistant answered. When she saw who it was, she invited him in. The doctor came when he was called.

"Ah squire! Good-day to you sir. I was about to come and see you. Your gamekeeper has a broken leg, and a very bruised and badly cut leg. You see both his legs are severely damaged. He'll be out of action for about six months, I'd say."

"When might I talk to him?" asked the squire.

"I would think tomorrow sometime — his head would have cleared by then. He must stay here for about a week, then I shall have to get him to his home to let his wife look after him."

"Very good doctor, I shall come back tomorrow, good-day to you."

The squire rode back to the Manor wondering what to do next. 'I believe the trouble with him is he's got it in for those Romanies. What a fool — they'll beat him every time. And of course they won't touch a pheasant in any case, that I know. Anyway, I shall see him tomorrow. I shall of course call on his wife this afternoon.'

At three o'clock sharp, the squire reined in outside of the keeper's cottage. He climbed down and knocked on the door with his riding crop. The keeper's wife came to answer the door. She was a neat little woman, and kept her cottage spotlessly clean.

"Good-day to 'ee squire," she said in her broad country accent.

"Good-day to you madam," replied the squire. "Might I have a word with you?"

"Yes of course sir, do come in."

The squire seated himself and the keeper's wife did the same.

"What can I do for you?" she asked.

"Well me dear, I've come about this accident that your husband has had."

"I keep wondering how it happened myself sir."

"Well apparently he stepped into the jaws of a mantrap. Now how the mantrap came to be there, I don't know. You see I do not allow those things on my estate. Supposing a little child walked into it."

"Oh my God sir, don't, I can't bear to think about it."

"Do you know my dear if the trap was his?"

"To tell you the truth sir, I don't ever remember seeing one — not ever. No, I don't think it belongs to him."

"Well my dear, because I can't prove that he set it, I can't sack him, but I must tell you this, he has only the Romanies to thank for saving his life. Had they not rescued him, he would have bled to death. However, I shall see him tomorrow. I shall keep him on, on half pay, until he is well enough to resume his duties. He must learn to respect those Romanies. You see, they are not poachers. Well, I must go now. Good-day my dear. I shall see you again."

"Thank you sir, and good-day."

The next day the squire rode to the doctor's house where he asked if he might see his keeper. He was ushered into a back room where the keeper lay on a bed.

"Well now Davis. What have you been doing?"

"Don't rightly know sir."

"Well, how the devil did you get caught in that trap?"

"Never saw it sir."

"Well then how do you think the trap got there?"

"Those gypsies sir, I reckon."

"Oh come off it man, they would never interfere with anything — they never have — why should they start now? If they did that sort of thing it would mean the end of their camping site. And don't you know they have saved your life?"

"I suppose they did in a way sir."

"Well of course they did man" replied the squire. "If they hadn't heard your cries for help you would have bled to death — that's according to the doctor of course. Now, are you telling the truth when you say that you didn't know how the trap got there?"

"Yes sir."

"Well I can assure you that the Romanies stay. They saved my father from being burned to death, plus a house full of his guests. That's why he gave them a permanent campsite on the common for life. Now you can see why I shall never have them moved. Do you understand me?"

"Yes sir."

"And remember, I will never have a mantrap on this estate. Never. I must tell you that I have seen your wife and explained to her as I am about to explain to you. Firstly I am not satisfied with the tales of how the trap got there in the first place, therefore I shall not sack you. However, being as you will be off sick for about six months, you are employed, but on half pay for the period you are sick. Now any more trouble with, or, about the Romanies, it will be the sack for you."

"Thank you sir," replied the keeper.

"Very well Davis, now you have plenty of time for reflection. Also the Romanies have handed in your muzzle-loader to me. It can stay in the gunroom until you are on duty again. Must be off now, I shall keep my eye on your progress."

With that the squire left. On his way out he saw the doctor putting up medicine.

"How is me keeper Doctor Jones?" he asked.

"Well sir, it's not as bad a break as I at first thought. It's like a piece of bone was smashed inwards by the jaws of the trap. I can have him on his feet in about one month, but I can't guarantee that he will be fit for work at that time."

"Did he say how it happened?"

"No, but the Romanies were saying to him, 'Serves you damn well right keeper for getting caught in your own bloody trap. You should remember where you set it. Put a signpost by it' suggested one."

How the squire laughed. "Well I suppose we shall never know. Let me have your bill, doctor. Must go now. Goodbye to you."

CHAPTER 4

One day, after keeper Davis was able to get about again, he took a walk to look through his spyglass at the Romany camp. 'I really hates that lot' he thought to himself. 'I knows it was they who broke my leg.'

He sat there on a stump watching for about half an hour. "Got it" he said to himself "now I knows what to do. If they was caught with one of squire's lambs up there — one of his best ones — ready for a feast or something. Yes. That's it. They would get thrown off the common on the spot, and for good."

Off he went making plans in his head to get them thrown out. First he would get a lamb; and it must be a nice one. He would take it up to the trees on the common's edge and hang it up ready for the supposed feast. Then he would go down to the Manor for the squire, collecting the head keeper as he went, and bring both the head keeper and the squire up to the common, and so catch the Romanies red-handed.

He chose a night when the moon was about half-full. Taking a length of rope he made his way over to the sheep pen. The sheep were all lying down quietly and peacefully. Looking out a nice lamb, he suddenly reached over the hurdles and grabbed it by the neck and a back leg. He managed to lift it out over the hurdles; it struggled and bleated pitifully. The other sheep got up and ran to the far side of the pen. Keeper took out his knife and cut the lamb's throat. It lay there on the ground kicking out its little life, and bleeding to death.

At last the lamb was still. Putting a rope loop around its back feet, he dragged it up across the field towards the Romany camp. It was all quiet as he approached.

However, Ned and his father had heard the sheep crying out, as

41

though a dog was upsetting them. So they crept down to the edge of the woods to listen. It was then that they saw the keeper dragging the lamb along in the moonlight.

"What the devil is he up to Pa'?"

"Don't know yet son, we'll just watch and see."

The keeper stopped several times to have a blow, and to look for signs of the Romanies. None. All was well. So he came boldly on. On reaching the trees he heaved the lamb up as high as he could by passing the rope over a branch. Satisfied with his work, he tied the rope securely, then scuttled away towards the head keeper's lodge as fast as he could go.

"Have you worked out what he's up to yet Pa'?"

"Well, I'm sure he's trying to get us into trouble, and he's off now to get the head keeper or someone. Now I've got a plan forming in my head. Perhaps we could work something out together. You go and round up the lads, and we'll see what we come up with."

Ned ran off and came back with Tosho, Owl and Madcap Jimmy King.

Pa' Jobey quickly explained what he and Ned had seen. "Now we must turn the tables on him before he can bring someone back here."

Before he could say anymore, Madcap shouted "Got it. How would it be if we took the lamb down and carried it to the keeper's shed and hung it up in there?"

"That's it," agreed Pa' Jobey. "Look, I need three men; two to carry the lamb tied on a pole, take it to his shed and hang it up tied to a beam; the other man must act as a scout to make sure the coast is clear as you go."

Owl, Ned and Madcap set about the job at once.

Now keeper Davies had run back to the head keeper's lodge and knocked him up, telling him that he had seen the Romanies kill a lamb and hang it on a tree ready for a feast. "It's there now" he explained. "Saw it with my own eyes."

"Well, I'm not going up there" replied the head keeper. "That's suicide."

"Well, shouldn't we get his lordship?" suggested keeper Davis.

"Yes, that's a good idea" agreeed the head keeper, "then he would see for himself wouldn't he?"

It was ten-thirty when the head keeper knocked on the door of the Manor. The butler came with a hand lamp asking what the trouble was. Keeper explained.

"His lordship is still up and reading" he replied. "I shall fetch him to you.''

His lordship came rather bad temperedly to the door. ''Now what's the trouble man calling me out at this time?''

Keeper explained.

''Rubbish!'' replied the squire.

But the keeper insisted, so squire made himself ready and left to go to the common to see for himself.

On arrival there was no one about. The under keeper took them to where he supposedly saw them hang the lamb. There was nothing there. No sign of it at all.

Jobey came now saying ''What's going on here then?''

''Have you seen a lamb hanging up here?'' asked the squire.

''A lamb sir! Shouldn't you see the shepherd about lambs?''

''Normally'' he replied, ''but my under keeper says he saw some men from here take a lamb and hang it on a tree just here.''

''Did he now'' replied Jobey.

Several men had gathered now and had formed a ring around them.

''Can I have a word privately?'' asked Jobey.

The squire agreed.

''Just watch those two only,'' said Jobey to the ring of men. ''I shall be back in a minute or two.''

Jobey took the squire out of earshot and told him all that had happened. How they heard the sheep bleating in terror over something. Then as they watched they saw the under keeper dragging the lamb up across the field in the moonlight to hang it on a tree. Then how they saw him scarper off as quickly as he could to the head keeper's lodge, and how they guessed what was happening, so they took down the lamb and carried it to keeper Davis's shed and hung it up in there.

''It's in there at this very moment sir. You should know full well we should never touch your things. But I must add after this I can't be responsible for your keeper's safety from now on should he come near here now, can I?''

''Right Jobey, leave it to me.''

The squire and Jobey went back to the group.

''Let 'em go men,'' ordered Jobey.

The ring of men melted away back among the shadows of the trees, while the squire and his two keepers departed.

*   *   *

''Where are we going sir?'' asked the head keeper.

''Down to keeper Davis's cottage to his shed'' replied the squire.

"Whatever for sir?" asked keeper Davis.

"We shall see when we get there," replied the squire.

No one spoke on the way back. At last they arrived at the shed. The squire called for a light. He held it up, and there for all to see was one of the squire's fat lambs.

"Now Davis, I have warned you several times about interfering with the Romanies. They will beat you every time. They beat you with your mantrap. I know that you set it up near their camp. Well they moved it back to your end of the footpath, so that one of their children wouldn't get caught in it. They even watched you set it man. They also saw you with the lamb, and they took it down and hung it in here. Now you have one week to get off my estate. You are sacked. Now get out of my sight. I did warn you once before and you failed to heed it. Now head keeper, take the lamb, cut it up, and distribute it among the old people on the estate. Good-night to you, and I hope you also have learned a lesson tonight."

The squire left for his bed.

'My God!' thought the head keeper 'it don't pay to upset those Romanies that's for sure, or they will darn soon put an end to the matter. Yes squire, I have learned a lesson tonight. Treat 'em with respect.'

It was sometime after the lamb episode — Old Jimmy Williams went one evening for a jug of ale and a chat down at the King's Arms Tavern. As he stood at the bar talking to landlord Bill Clover, three of the squire's estate workers (joskins) came in. They took a jug of ale each, and sat at a table.

The landlord asked them if they wanted any Murphys. Yes, they did. The landlord's wife always cooked trays of baked potatoes for the bar. Just before they were cooked, she would pierce them well with a fork, then pour rum over them, and bake them for a further five to ten minutes. Needless to say they were very popular with the customers, who would eat them hot or cold, and really seemed to enjoy them, especially with butter.

As the evening wore on, Jimmy Williams, the vardo builder, was about to say good-night to the landlord, when peals of drunken laughter and loud talk from the joskins' table made him wait awhile. They were discussing the fact that if they wanted more ale all they needed to do was to poach the squire's game, sell it, and blame its disappearance on the Romanies. They all seemed at this hour the worse for drink, and were talking quite loudly and boastfully. The gist of their talk was that at full moon they would go out and poach the squire's game, and put the blame on the Romanies. One said "We got old keeper Davis on our side, he hates those people.''

Jim waited no longer, he went off home to tell his daughter Clare of what was afoot. She offered to ride up to the common next day to alert the Romanies as to what was going to happen at full moon. Her father agreed.

The very next day, she saddled her horse and rode off up to the common gate. Two men appeared.

"What do you want?'' they asked.

She replied "I'm the daughter of Jim Williams the vardo builder. I need to see someone in the Doe family.''

They let her in and pointed the way. She rode in among the trees until she spotted Ma' Marti cleaning her vardo steps. She asked Ma' where she could find her husband or the boys, because she had vital news for them. Ma' escorted her to the men and listened to what she had to say.

"So the joskins want a war eh! Tell your father that we shall take care of it, and thank him from me for telling us'' replied Pa' Jobey.

Ma' gave Clare a hot drink and she sat talking to Rikkeni for quite some time. After saying goodbye she raced off, taking the gate in her stride.

Arriving home, she told her father all that had happened, then added rather disappointedly "I never saw Ned.''

That evening as the family gathered around the fire, Madcap came to visit the Doe brothers, as he did most evenings.

"Now'' explained Jobey, "I want everybody's attention because I got important news.''

Everyone fell quiet and the leg-pulling stopped. Pa' Jobey explained about the message that Clare had brought; that the squire's joskins (farm labourers) were going to poach his game from the estate and put the blame on the Romanies. "Jimmy Williams, the vardo builder, overheard them talking when they were almost drunk in the tavern. That's why he sent his daughter Clare up here to warn us. Now I wants an eye kept on these joskins because they plan to do it at full moon; then we shall get the blame.''

"Don't worry Pa' Jobey, as soon as we see 'em we'll go down there and bash 'em up'' suggested Madcap, jumping up and sparring about. "First a left, then a right. Boom! Boom!''

"Alright Madcap, sit down a minute. First we must catch 'em red-handed, then we must plan according to the situation'' explained Pa'.

From that moment on, the lads would watch each night as the moon grew, and listen for any trouble with the squire's game birds.

It was about full moon. A clear frosty period had set in. Owl noticed as he came home from Tisbury that two men were hedge trimming beside the road. A watch was kept on these men. Halfway through the afternoon, they were seen setting rabbit snares, which they had no right to do, because of the squire's game birds getting caught in them.

As darkness fell, Jobey felt sure that tonight they would strike. After supper was eaten, the lads spread out and kept watch over a wide area. Their orders were, as soon as they saw anything they were to return to Pa' Jobey, who would give his owl call. This would mean that the poachers had been spotted, and they must all come into camp for fresh orders.

It happened at eight o'clock that night. Tosho had spotted three men on the south side of the covert. There the pheasants were roosting away from the cold north-east wind. He came quietly back to Pa' Jobey to report what he had seen.

Pa' gave his owl call, and very soon the others who were out scouting came running back to camp. Pa' explained the situation and said, "First we must wait until they have taken a fair bit of game. Then we've got 'em red-handed."

Madcap and Ned were sent to watch the poachers. Yes, there they were. They had long slender poles which looked a good twelve-foot long. On the small end of these they had a rabbit snare. They were putting the poles up in the trees carefully getting the nooses over the birds' heads. Then quickly pulling them off their roosts they pulled the birds' necks, and put them in a sack. Resetting their snares, they would repeat the process. The two spy scouts watched until the poachers had a good haul.

"Let's do 'em now Ned" suggested Madcap.

"No, better do as Pa' said or I shall get into trouble."

At last the poachers seemed to be well pleased with their haul, and decided now to visit their rabbit snares. Off they went carrying their long catching poles and their sack of game birds.

The two lads went quickly back to Jobey to report. They could see the poachers spread out across the field in the moonlight taking rabbits from their snares. Suddenly, and without any warning, three horsemen appeared in the moonlight racing straight at them. The poachers started to run in terror from these night riders. But the horses that were bearing down on them quickly closed. As they did so, the poachers were knocked to the ground by a mighty blow on the back of their heads. The riders were carrying an old sock each, with several handfuls of wet earth in the toe, which they were whirling around their heads and yelling like madmen. A good blow from this weapon had stunned the joskin poachers and knocked them flat.

Pa' Jobey and Madcap ran out of the trees and waded into them as they staggered to their feet. The riders turned and came racing back to join in the fight, throwing themselves from their horses, they soon overpowered the poaching joskins. Their faces looked a sorry mess. They had bleeding noses and mouths, with eyes closing rapidly.

Madcap was still sparring about shouting "Come on you thieving joskins, fight. Let's have you. I'll take on all three of you at once."

Pa' Jobey told Ned to ride to the South Lodge and fetch the head keeper (cannie-moosh), then on to the Manor House for the squire (boro-rye) himself. Jobey was determined to end it tonight once and for all, so that the world would know that you can't put on the Romanies and get away with it.

Ned came racing through the night to the keeper's lodge. He was off his horse and running for the door even before the horse had stopped. He banged loudly.

The keeper came with a lighted candle shouting "What's all this about then?"

Ned explained that they had caught three of the squire's joskins poaching his game.

"Where?" asked the keeper.

"In the big common field" replied Ned.

"Don't be daft" said the keeper, "they will be miles away by now."

"I'll tell you this much" replied Ned, "if you don't go and bring them in, they could be dead by morning with that wild bunch looking after 'em. I'm going for the squire right now. Cheerio."

He leapt on his horse and went hell for leather across the park to the Manor House where he banged loudly on the door. The butler came saying "What's so urgent then?"

"Must see squire — it's very urgent" replied Ned.

"He won't be pleased mind" replied the butler.

"Can't help that" retorted Ned. "Must see him."

He was led off to see the squire where he explained to him what had happened that evening.

"Where are they now?" asked the squire.

"Waiting for you sir."

"But surely they would have gone home by now?"

"Our men will never let them go, only on your orders. They are quite safe and tied up sir. All waiting for you."

The squire asked the exact location of the poachers.

Ned explained.

"Alright my boy, I shall be there as soon as my horse is ready."

Ned came racing back to the field and told Pa' Jobey what had happened. "The gamekeeper and the squire were on their way."

The three joskins were lying on their stomachs with their hands tied behind their backs. The rope from their hands was passed back to their feet and pulled tight. Madcap was still prancing up and down looking for a fight, continually challenging all three of them at once. He was very excited. Pa' Jobey simply laughed at him and refused to untie the joskins, while Owl and Tosho watched their captives closely, sticks (coshes) in their hands; their horses stood nearby, heads drooping, waiting patiently. They could hear a pony and jingle coming along the gravel road now, in the quiet frosty moonlit night; while farther back, and still hidden in a belt of mist, they could clearly hear a lone rider trotting at a fast pace.

The pony and jingle came in through the field gate and across the field to where the poachers were held. The driver spotted them and came towards them. It was the head keeper.

"What's going on here then?" he asked.

"There's your poachers" replied Jobey "complete with their haul."

At this point the squire came galloping up in the moonlight. "Ah!" he exclaimed. "Mr Jobey Doe eh? And what's being going on here Jobey?"

"Can I have a word sir to answer your question?"

"Certainly" replied the squire.

Jobey took the squire to one side and told him what was overheard in the tavern, and because of that they had kept their eyes open, just in case it might be true; and tonight they had caught the poachers.

"Well done Jobey! Very good thinking indeed. Now get your men to make them stand up so that I can see them. I need to recognize them you see."

"Get 'em up on their feet men," shouted Jobey.

They were hauled up very roughly to their feet, while the squire and his keeper walked along identifying them. Yes, they were all estate farm workers (joskins).

"And what have you got to say for yourselves?" bellowed the squire.

No one spoke.

"What have they poached, head keeper?" he asked.

"Twelve pheasants, three hares, and eight rabbits," he replied.

"So you thought that you could poach my game, and blame the Romanies for taking it? Eh! What! All I can say to you is that you are bloody fools, which by the look of you, you have already found out. I should hand you over to the law and have you flogged. However, by the state of your faces I would say that you have already received your punishment in full. Never underestimate a Romany. These people are my friends. They are to be left in peace or else. Now for poaching my game, which I have paid keeper to rear and protect, you are sacked from this moment on. Be off my land by Monday morning, or the law will take its course. Untie their hands men.''

The joskins were set free, and were told to get off the estate; whereupon they took to their heels and ran for their lives, wanting to get as far away from those Romanies as possible.

"Now look here you chaps, you have shown great presence of mind and loyalty to me. I am extremely pleased with you. Now take this game as a token of my gratitude and have a damn good feed. Now as for you keeper, should you ever get troubled with poachers, all you have to do is to send for Mr Jobey Doe and his merry men. Thank you chaps, now I really must go, me supper's getting cold you see. Good-night now.''

The squire mounted his horse and rode away. The keeper followed suit, taking the poachers' catching snares and poles with him.

"Well, you heard the squire" said Jobey, "come on let's go and have a damn good supper.''

Madcap just danced with joy saying "Come on let's go look for more poachers, men.''

They invited all the people in the camp to a real beano the very next night to celebrate 'the fall of the joskins'.

The Last Contraband Run

CHAPTER 5

One morning the family set out on yet another contraband run. Little did they know of the excitement in store for them. They arrived at King Henry's Barn as usual. The journey being normal and uneventful.

On the very first night there, at one-thirty in the morning to be exact, the ponies arrived with the kegs of brandy. Nothing was expected at this time. However, the kegs were loaded into the solivardo for quickness, and covered with a green sailcloth.

"Move out soon mind" advised the pony men as they hurriedly left the campsite.

Next morning the family moved out very early, intending to travel until dark. At about three o'clock in the afternoon, Ned, who was riding ahead as scout, came back to Pa' Jobey to report that he had seen about ten soldiers marching along behind a horse and wagon.

"Where are they now?" he asked.

"Over by that big chalk-pit" replied Ned, "where we used to camp."

"We'll camp to the left of that in the woods tonight Ned. We should be about half a mile away from them at least. I'll find a spot, you tell the others to pull in behind me."

This they did. A fire was started and a meal cooked. The horses were fed and watered, but the solivardo was pushed by hand into a large area of rhododendrons and camouflaged, because it contained the whole consignment of brandy.

Just as it was getting dark, and the family had almost eaten their meal, there came a disturbance from the horses. The boys ran to see what was upsetting them. They found some foot-soldiers and a sergeant looking them over. The horses didn't like them at all.

"What's the trouble here?" asked Ned.

"We need your horses" replied the sergeant.

"Better see Pa' about that" suggested Ned.

"And where might he be?" replied the sergeant.

"Just through there, eating his supper" came the answer.

"Supper 'aye. Let's go and see men."

The soldiers left to see Pa', while the lads calmed the frightened horses. When they did get back to the wagon area, they heard raised voices.

"Get your hands off my daughter you bastard" shouted Pa' Jobey.

"Calm down old man" said the sergeant. "We are only going to borrow her for the night. You can have her back again tomorrow, a bit the worse for wear maybe, but she will be back."

The lads were horrified. There stood the soldiers, leering all over their faces, while the sergeant held on to Rikkeni.

"This is the last time I shall tell you. Let her go" demanded Jobey.

The sergeant laughed aloud in Pa's face and said, "Come on lads, let's go, we got all we need."

But, at that moment, Pa' Jobey let go a real haymaker, catching the sergeant full in the mouth. He went flying backwards, stunned and bleeding badly from his badly damaged lips and nose.

He let go of Rikkeni at once. She ran straight to her vardo and slammed the door. Ma' Marti immediately grabbed a carving knife and defied anyone to go near her. (And no one did.)

All this time, the lads hid watching. Their presence would have been no use in this situation at the moment. Pa' Jobey had seen them in the bushes and knew their thoughts.

It was growing dark now as the sergeant staggered to his feet. "Bring him" he said, pointing at Pa' and spitting out blood and teeth. "I'll deal with him later."

The men took Pa' and trundled him along making their way back into the woods.

"You two stay here" whispered Ned. 'I'll follow to see where they are taking him. Leave the solivardo where it is, but get ready to move out. I'll be back as soon as I can.

Ned followed the soldiers through the woods like a panther, until they came to an open glade where there were two tents erected near a fire. Standing by it was a soldier cooking. Pa' noticed all this as he was taken to a birch tree on the far side of the glade, where his hands were tied behind his back and also to the tree.

Ned worked his way around behind his father.

"It's me Pa' — Ned," he whispered.

Taking his knife, he cut his father's bonds.

"Listen Ned, I'll stay here and act as though I am still tied up, you go and get the boys, because I have a plan."

Pa' simply stayed where he was, his hands behind his back as though he was still tied to the tree, and waiting on the sergeant's pleasure. Ned ran back for his brothers as Pa' had instructed. The soldiers' meal was almost ready. They would be eating soonest, as anyone could tell. They were not interested in Jobey at this time.

The sergeant was having his face seen to by the medical orderly. When the orderly had finished, the sergeant shouted across to Pa', "I'll deal with you after supper, Mister Bastard. For now you can stay in the frost and freeze, you old devil."

After a while, the boys came creeping up behind Pa' in the undergrowth.

"Now listen carefully all of you. Just down the track to the right over there is that big old chalk-pit where we used to camp. Now you see the moon rising, well very soon that bank of mist will rise from the pit and cover the top edge of it like it did before. Do you remember?"

"Yeah, we remember Pa'."

Now I want two of you to go down there and move those sheep hurdles from along the top edge. They are there to stop people and animals from falling in. Now you put them on each side out of the way, and out of sight. When the bank of mist has risen, and it completely covers the chalk-pit from view, I want to hear your owl call. Hide yourselves on each side of the trackway in the mist, with a good cosh in your hands. Now the third man must come to the end of the glade, down there, and demand that I be set free. Now, they will, if I'm not mistaken, get up and chase after him on the sergeant's orders, of course. Now as you can see, this man is a toll-bird. He must run like hell into the bank of mist then jump to one side. Now these troops don't know about that pit. They will all charge into the mist bank, only to drop forty foot into that blackthorn thicket, that's growing below in the old pit bottom. Have you got that?"

The boys loved the plan. "You're on Pa' " they agreed. "We like it." They smacked palms and crept away.

It took about fifteen minutes before Jobey heard the owl call. 'T'a, Wit, T'a, Whooo.' The next thing he heard was "Hi! You bastards! What are you doing with my father? Let him go at once damn you." There stood Tosho demanding his father's release in a very unfriendly way.

The sergeant was furious. "Damn that little bastard" he shouted, "he's followed us here. A quart of ale to the man who can grab him."

Up jumped the soldiers, and went racing after Tosho, led by the sergeant. He kept just ahead of them letting them think that they would catch him at any minute. They came trampling along behind him like a herd of cattle. Straight into the mist ran Tosho. It hung like a huge blanket across the chalk-pit. Tosho dived to one side and was caught by Ned. He had almost misjudged it. But the troopers came racing blindly on, knowing no difference. Straight over the edge of the steep pit they went, blinded by that thick screen of mist. Yes, over they all went, sergeant and all. Their cries and screams of terror rent the still frosty night air. One man who was behind all the others managed to stop short of the pit. He just stood there staring into its great depth in disbelief. As he stood there looking in, he received a mighty bash across the back of his head, which sent him flying headlong into the pit on top of his comrades, whose moans and groans went completely unheeded by the Romanies.

The brothers, having accomplished their part of the plan, went back to see how Pa' Jobey was coping. They found him taking down the two tents.

"What's to do now Pa'?" they asked.

"Well, he's taken care of replied Pa' " pointing to the tied up guard. "What's happened to the others?"

"All in the pit as your orders were" replied Ned.

"Right my lads, there's work to do. I want all their kit thrown on that wagon; those muskets that are stacked in a pile over there as well."

Everything was put on the wagon.

"Now what?" asked Ned.

"Push the wagon over the fire" replied Jobey.

This they did. The fire was built up to burn fiercely. The horse was unharnessed. The harness was also put on the fire, while the horse was turned loose to fend for itself. The guard was dragged along by his feet and thrown into the pit with his chums. Then the sheep hurdles were re-erected once more to stop anyone from falling into that dangerous pit.

"That's taught that cocky sergeant a lesson I reckon" said Pa' Jobey, as they hurried back to Ma' and Rikkeni.

The vardos were ready to move. All they had to do was to fetch the solivardo from the bushes.

A loud boom made everyone stop and look. "It's only their gunpowder keg gone up" explained Pa', laughing.

Soon they were under way, travelling all night. At daybreak they came to where the road forked. Now Pa', seeing two men who had just set about the job of cutting a tree, had an idea to lay a false trail; so he pulled up and asked, "Which is the Salisbury road, matey?'' The man pointed, so Jobey took the Salisbury road.

About a mile further on, he knew that he could cut back through and come out on the Tisbury road again; therefore anyone following them would go chasing off to Salisbury; but Jobey and family would be on the Tisbury road.

When they were back on the road for home once again, Pa' called a halt. While Ma' and Rikkeni made a quick meal, the lads attended to the horses. After a few hours' rest, they changed their wagon horses, or as the Romanies would say they (chopped the groi). On again, now, to arrive on the common safely at dusk.

Madcap came to make himself useful; so he was given the job of lighting the fire.

The family soon settled in. After a quick meal, Ned went off to Tisbury to see if there were any troopers about. None anywhere. Back to report to Pa' Jobey, who decided to drive the solivardo himself down to the tavern.

This he did; the kegs were soon unloaded and put down in Bill Clover's secret cellar in the stables.

Jobey went into Bill's back kitchen. There he was told that word had come to him that very morning by means of a letter sent down on the stage-coach. It stated that the ship that did the contraband run from France to England, had been captured by two frigates belonging to HM Navy.

"The captured ship was full of contraband, so Jobey my friend it looks as though you have just done your last trip.''

"Thank God for that,'' replied Jobey.

He then told Bill Clover about the trouble they had this time with the troopers.

"Well, you see,'' replied Bill, "they were ordered to co-operate with the navy at sea, and the custom's men on the coast. You were lucky Jobey.''

But when Jobey explained how they had ditched the troopers into the old chalk-pit, Bill Clover just fell about rolling in agonies of laughter.

"You've made my day Jobey, you old devil, you really have. You're a man after me own heart, and you fair made my belly 'ake.''

The very next day while the Doe family were resting up, Jobey told them all that they had just finished their last run. Everyone was very pleased about that. Madcap came at that point. He had been to Tisbury to take some of his wood carvings to the shop. He had also called into the tavern. Bill Clover had two gents in there asking for lodgings for two or three days.

"You just passing through?" asked Bill.

"It's roughly like that" they replied. "We are surveying for the Railroad Company. It will run from London to Salisbury; from there on down to Exeter to connect the West Country with the capital. The railroad is already under way from London to Salisbury.

"I overheard everything" explained Madcap. "Anyway, Bill sent them over to the forge. The smith always knows where they can stay and where they can stable their horses. Oh! Yes! Listen to this, Bill also told me that the old boro-rye (squire) had been taken very ill."

"Well if he dies" replied Jobey, "we could be thrown off the common that's for sure."

"What shall we do Pa'?" asked Ma' Marti.

"Well Ma', I've been thinking coming home this time. We are fairly rich now, also we are getting older. Now I figures that we should get a small farm for the horses, and for ourselves, as a permanent home. We owe it to the boys and Rikkeni. You see Ma', what nearly happened to Rikkeni out there on the downs, fair upset me. God knows I don't get upset very much. So what do you think Ma'?"

"You mean live like a gorgio" (house dweller).

"Yeah. Something like that."

"Pa' Jobey! Keep your eye open for a place that's my answer."

Pa' was happy now, because Ma' counted very much with the family. Yes, she would always carry the day. He put the idea to the family at the next mealtime. To his surprise they didn't seem to mind at all.

*   *   *

About a week later, Ma' came out of her vardo looking very worried.

"What's up Ma'?" asked Jobey.

"I just seen something terrible in my crystal ball" she replied.

"Like what?" he asked.

"I think the old squire is going to die very soon. I saw his funeral."

The next morning all the Romanies, numbering a crowd of forty to fifty people, assembled on the lawn of the Manor House. The old squire had his bed downstairs. He ordered it to be turned and put near the window, so that he could see all his old friends.

This was done. They all stayed for about two hours. Then Ma' Marti announced in a loud voice "It's all over". So they all walked away and left the Manor.

The doctor came to the squire's bed to check his pulse. There was none at all. He was dead.

As the Romanies left the Manor House lawn, so the old squire had died. They had paid their last respects. Ned went down to the village to see Clare for a while. When he was there he talked to her father telling him that the old squire was dead.

"It means trouble for you I reckon, Ned," replied Jimmy Williams.

"Yeah. Pa' wants to buy a farm" replied Ned. "Not a big one you understand, but big enough for horse dealing, you know."

"Wait a minute. There's a chap out on the Swallow-Cliff road by the name of Legg. He's selling out, or trying to. That's according to the smith mind. Why don't you call at the forge on your way home and find out?"

As Ned went home to supper, he saw the smith and asked him if it was true — 'Yes it was'.

The smith gave him all the details that he knew, and advised that Jobey should go over and see Mr Legg. Ned went racing off home to tell Pa'. He would go and see. Both he and Ma' would take the solivardo and go first thing tomorrow.

Ned was very quiet at breakfast, as Ma' and Pa' went off to see Mr Legg.

It ended up that Pa' Jobey had bought the farm. It was fifty-five acres, with a three acre wood. There was a good big six-bedroomed farmhouse, cow pens, stables, and two barns. They would move there in three weeks.

*   *   *

For several days now, Ned seemed to be quiet and upset.

One day his mother said "You got troubles haven't you son?"

"Nothing you can help with Ma'," he replied.

"Try me" she suggested.

"Well Ma' if you must know, I was going to ask Clare to marry me, now I can't."

"Why ever not?" asked Ma'.

"Well, because we are related that's why."

"Of course you aren't related" replied Ma'.

"Oh yes we are. Dad's mother's sister was her mother or something."

"No!" replied Ma'. "There was a relation that he was married to, but she died at childbirth, the baby as well. Then Jimmy married again; but not to anyone related to us. Clare's mother died, yes, but she was no relation to us at all. Neither was her mother. Poor old Jimmy'' said Ma', reflectively.

Ned's face lit up. "Then I can marry Clare after all?"

"Of course you can son. Didn't you know?"

He let out a wild yell as the good news dawned on him.

Ned raced for his horse, leapt on its back and went streaking off down the long gravel road to Tisbury. She watched him go with some amusement, as she listened to his wild yells of excitement, as he dashed along at a breakneck speed.

He rushed in to Clare and told her the news.

"I didn't know that" she replied.

"Go ask your dad" he suggested.

This she did, only to come running back saying "'Tis true Ned. 'Tis true.''

Ned wasted no more time. He took her in his arms and asked her to marry him. She immediately said 'Yes. Yes. Yes'. Off went Ned, promising to see her that evening. Clare was happy now. And Ned was as high as the moon with excitement.

CHAPTER 6

The days were slipping by now, and the family were anxiously waiting to be able to move into the farm that Pa' Jobey had bought with the proceeds of running the contraband brandy. It would enable them to have a permanent home for all time, and it was to be at the place known as Bunter's Farm.

At last the agreed day arrived. Owl was told to ride over to see if the previous owner had left the premises. He returned within the hour to announce that the farm was completely empty.

The family had packed up their worldly goods, and were waiting ready to move out. Off they went with the spare horses tied on behind the backs of their wagons. Madcap was coming along to see where they were going to live; then he could visit sometimes. Ned was pleased to be going, because he would be much nearer to his lady-love.

Down the long winding gravel road they made their way, with the horses' hooves and the wagon wheels rattling out their approach.

"Here it is Rikkeni" explained Ma' at last, as Pa', who was driving the leading wagon followed Ned and Madcap, who had turned off the road now, and were going up the lane that led to the farm.

Into the yard at last they all came. Ma' and Rikkeni went into the house to have a look around. Quite a lot of furniture had been left in there because the old couple were going to live at Hindon with their married daughter. Her husband did not return from a trip to sea with HM Navy, therefore all the furniture they would need had been supplied by their daughter. Ma' Marti was pleased to have the furniture, it would start them off as gorgios.

Pa' Jobey soon had a fire going in the big kitchen for Ma', while the boys checked a paddock behind the barn, making sure that the fences were good enough to turn the horses out in.

The vardo wagons were unloaded and pushed back into an empty barn for repainting. While Rikkeni unpacked the cooking utensils, Ma' and Pa' took the solivardo to go shopping in Tisbury.

The boys returned with five shoshies (rabbits) which were caught by the lurchers. They were very pleased to be able to catch shoshies on their own land. The dogs were given a nice strawed up bed in the empty pigsties. They seemed to like this, and were soon stretched out on the clean straw sleeping soundly.

Ma' Marti came back now to organize the place her way, while Jobey carried in several lots of shopping.

At last it was organized, and everything was underway. Madcap wanted to rent an empty shed where he could do his wood carving in peace. It was in fact the old dairy cakehouse. It even had an old open fireplace for heating his glue.

"Well now" explained Jobey, "being as we are all gorgios (house dwellers), yes you can have it; after all you were brought up with the boys and you won't want to leave them now will you?"

"No Pa', you see there is only mother and me, and we shall find it hard if we have to leave the common."

"Well Madcap, just up the lane near the woods are two old cottages. They need a bit of doing up. Now if you cared to put your carving skills to work and do one up, you and your Ma' could live there quite happily I reckon; then you would be a gorgio like us — in the warm and dry, for your old Ma'.

Madcap dashed off to see the old cottages. Within half an hour he was back.

"Can I have the use of the garden as well Pa'?" he asked.

"Of course it goes with the cottage. Mind you it seems that nobody has lived there for about three years.

He grabbed hold of Pa's hand, and slapped palms in agreement, then ran from the kitchen and rode off towards the common at quite a fast pace.

*　　*　　*

Ned and Owl had decided to share out their haul from the Manor security box. They had taken it as payment for Ned and Clare's imprisonment, when Ned was locked up in the cellars by the evil butler.

"Now that the boro-rye (Lord of the Manor, or Squire) is dead, he won't want what we've borrowed" decided Ned. "So I think the time is right to share it out. What do you say pal (brother)?"

"Yeah, I reckon now's the time," agreed Owl.

From under the floor of the solivardo they took out their haul.

"Go fetch Pa' " suggested Ned. "Then we can explain how we got it."

There were several necklaces; one was a real dazzler. He put that back in his pocket, that was for Clare; also a beautiful ring.

Pa' came with Owl now. When he saw the loot laid out on the lid of the corn-bin he asked, "Where did that lot come from?"

"Easy Pa' " replied Ned. "If you listen I will explain."

"Go ahead" demanded Pa'.

Ned set to and reminded Pa' of the time he was locked up in the prison cell in the old Manor House cellar; of how the butler moosh (man) explained when he brought Ned a meal, which was carried in by Clare while the butler held a gun on him, that he had to have his meal now because all the fires were being left to go out so that the sweep's boy could climb the chimneys and clean them all while the squire was away.

"It was after the meal, you see Pa', as I sat back on my little wooden bunk, that I remembered what old Grandad Amos once said. He told me 'that the rich people always kept their valuables hidden behind the firebacks of large old fireplaces, never letting the fire go out', like the one in the hall at the Manor House. Now as luck would have it, later that night Owl and Madcap got me out, thanks to Bill Clover and his scheming ways. After we got out in the park I could see how easy it was to get back into the Manor. Now Owl and me we nipped back into the Manor saying that we had left something behind. While the others waited, we crept in, opened the fireback and helped ourselves. You see Pa' that was sometime ago now, and the evil old butler who locked me up, and kept Clare a prisoner for three years, was given penal servitude for life for taking the squire's valuables. Well of course as you can see they have funnily enough turned up right here, so I reckon that if you came to see fair play, we could safely divide it up between the family."

Jobey looked, scratched his head, then said "I'm buggered if I know about you lot, you're all worse than me. But I must say good thinking on your part son. Then he went into fits of laughter. "Yes. You're a chip off the old block alright. I've got to admit son, it's a good time to share it out I can tell you, because I'm pretty well stretched to buy this place, which as you know I had to do."

"Right come on then Pa', let's get sharing."

It worked out at two hundred guineas each for all six members of the family. There was extra for Ned and Owl, and some was put aside for Madcap; he had earned his share by showing sheer guts whenever he was needed. He was like a member of the family really.

However, Pa' decided that the necklaces should be put away for a good while yet. Just to be on the safe side, everyone was sworn to secrecy — then they were given their share. How happy they all were as they sat around in the kitchen drinking tea (meski). Now they were all set for life. If a man had a hundred guineas in those days, he was rich.

Now they could buy stock for the farm. Ma' Marti wanted some hens and a few goats or a cow (dunnik).

They were all planning away, when they heard a wagon coming up the lane. Tosho went to see who it was through the open window. There, coming up the lane was Madcap, riding his horse bareback as usual; followed by Ma' King who was sat up on the seat driving her vardo, and happily smoking her pipe (swegler), blowing out clouds of tobacco smoke (toovalo), which was being wafted away by the light breeze.

Everyone came out to give them a cheer. Madcap waved and bowed to them, but old Ma' King didn't even 'bat an eyelid' as the saying goes. She simply stared straight ahead and kept going.

How the Doe family laughed. Yes, they were highly amused.

*　　*　　*

That evening Ned went over to Long Barn to see Clare. As they sat talking, Clare's father came in for a cup of tea (meski).

"Now you two" he asked. "When are you going to get married?"

"As soon as we can find somewhere to live" answered Clare. "We want somewhere near here so that I can look after you for always."

"Don't mind me," replied her father, "I can take care of myself."

"Then we won't get married" replied Clare, "and that's our decision."

"Well, I can't stay and argue, because I've got two men coming who wants to buy a vardo. Must go now."

Off went Jimmy out to his barn to await the two men's arrival. He hadn't long to wait. The two men drove up in a pony and trap with a horse tied on behind, all ready harnessed up to pull the vardo. Ned and Clare watched from the window as the men pulled up in the yard. They jumped down from the trap and walked towards the new vardo. This enabled Ned to get a good view of them.

"What's the matter Ned?" asked Clare, as she saw his face suddenly change.

"I don't like those two devils."

"What do you mean?" she asked.

"Well my dear, they are didakais. And those two are known as people who have never paid for anything in their lives, and I don't see them doing so now, not even for your father's vardo. Now look Clare can you let me out of your front door? Then I can run along behind the wall and get to the yard gate, and the rear of the barn if necessary, just in case they try to be funny."

"Be careful Ned," she warned.

"Look, I must do it in case they get rough with your dad, but I'll be careful" he promised.

She opened the door, and Ned bending low, ran along behind the garden wall. He reached the gate at the end of the wall. The men were laughing with old Jimmy at this point, but Ned was not deterred by this. He heard the men suggest that they should try and see if they could harness their horse into the new vardo. 'We might not have the right harness you see.' They tried their horse in the shafts, and harnessed it up perfectly. Ned watched and listened like a hawk.

The man who stood by the vardo's horse said, "Alf will pay you what we owe Mr Williams. Yeah, let's go into the barn then I can pay you and count it out on your table."

He followed Mr Williams into the barn. Ned was listening through the weather-boarding of the barn wall.

"Now listen you old fool" said the man, who was referred to as Alf. "Get wise to yourself. We ain't paying you a damn penny for that wagon."

"Then you don't take it" snapped Jimmy Williams.

"Thought so," muttered Ned to himself. His hand had closed around an old broken besom handle. This would do if he needed a cosh.

At that moment, he heard some thumping and a groan. "Right Joe, I got the old bugger. Let's tie him up and get out of here."

The two men were now in the barn tying up poor old Jimmy, so Ned closed the yard gate that led into the road. Creeping along the wall, he edged his way to the barn door. Peeping in, he knew the time was now or never, so he rushed in and felled one man with a blow to the head, and with one mighty swing he cracked the other fellow as he turned, right across his bottom jaw. He dropped beside his mate with a groan. Ned quickly untied old Jimmy and dragged him to the door. Dipping his hand in a water-butt, he wetted old Jimmy's face. He came to now moaning, then realizing where he was and what was going on, he tried to stand up.

"It's alright Jimmy. I got 'em," Ned assured him.

Jimmy's head was clearing now. "Good work Ned. Good

work," he mumbled again.

Clare came running — she could wait no longer. She knew there was trouble. If they had harmed her father she would scratch their eyes out. He had had his troubles in life without these two devils causing him more.

"You alright Dad?" she asked.

"I'm fine," he told her, "thanks to Ned. Now Clare if you want to help just unharness their horse from that vardo and open the yard gate."

She hastened to obey.

One man was stirring now. Ned shoved his boot into him and said "Get up!"

When the man had cleared his head he got to his feet. "Who are you mister?" he asked.

"I'm this man's friend" he replied. "Now take your partner and get out of here. My advice to you is get out and stay out, and above all don't come back, or you will be shot next time."

The man tried to wake his partner, but ended up trying to drag him over to the pony and trap. Ned grabbed one of his legs and dragged him over. He helped the man to throw him in the trap. He was moaning now and would soon wake up.

Ned tied the other horse to the back of their trap. "Right take it away" he ordered.

The man still dazed, and holding his head, climbed up to his seat, took the reins, and the pony trotted off down the road and across the green, while the man coming round in the back was still trying to stand. As the three standing at Long Barn gate watched, he did manage to stand, only to fall headlong, crashing out over the back to lie spread-eagled on the grass, being almost trampled on by the spare horse trotting behind. The man who was driving stopped and helped his very unsteady friend back into the trap. By this time the three at the farm gate were doubled up with laughter watching it all. As for poor old Jimmy, he had a sore jaw and some bruised ribs — but it would soon wear off.

"Thanks for your help young Ned."

"Oh that's alright, it was a pleasure" replied Ned. "I like a bit of fun. You see I happened to see them arrive through the window. I knew who they were, so Clare let me out of the front door. I ran along behind the garden wall and came up behind the barn just in time to shut the gate and catch 'em with me cosh."

They went indoors now, to get old Jim a cup of willow-bark tea to help his aching head.

As they sat there drinking meski (tea), old Jimmy said "Look here you two. Why don't you get married and take this place over?

You Ned would be a big help to me. Look what you have just done by recognizing those two didakais.''

"Yeah, Jimmy, but you see it's your place, and the feeling you have of it ever being yours again would be gone. I can't see it working out. We'll find a place of our own near here soon.''

"Look Ned, I lost her for three years and never expected to see her ever again, and it's only because she thought the world of me. You see son, I can't bear the thought of losing her again, she must have gone through hell. Well I'm just as unselfish as her. Put it this way, I won't have her happiness blighted just because of me. Therefore I shall will this place over to you both jointly, with effect from today. We've got five big rooms downstairs, and six up, so I reckon we three can live here — it's plenty big enough — we can work it out together. Now come on you two, give me your answer?''

"Yes Dad, we can sort it out.''

And so it was arranged.

There were six fields that went with Long Barn Farm. Ned could have their use for as long as he lived for his horses or whatever. All Jimmy wanted was the barn and two downstairs rooms, which was all he ever occupied anyway; and Clare would be on hand to look after him for ever, as long as he lived.

Now the wedding could be arranged. Ned went dashing off home to talk to his mother. She was pleased as she heard the news, and would see to all the arrangements herself.

* * *

The wedding plans were going ahead now. The vicar (tompad) would come up to Bunter's Farm, and the wedding would be held in the big barn. All their friends received an invite. There would be three fiddlers or violinists (boshomengros) coming to play their music for the dancers at the wedding feast (boro-divvas).

Everything went well. There was nothing unusual, it was a straightforward Christian wedding. But however, after the ceremony there came the old traditional Romany marriage ceremony, where the blood of both people are mingled to make them one person.

The vicar (tompad), who knew these people well, asked if he might stop and watch the Romany wedding ceremony, because he had never seen one. His wish was of course granted. The seats were placed around in the shape of a huge horseshoe. The guests were ushered to the seats — then it all started.

Standing there to give away Ned was Ma' Marti, and to give

away Clare was Ma' King; she was going to do it because of old Jimmy's wooden leg. The two women stood facing each other in the circle. They held their hands high reaching forward until their hands touched. They sprang apart now as Ned came between them from one side, and Clare from the other. Ma' King pricked the inside of Clare's left wrist until the blood came, while Ma' Marti did the same to Ned's left wrist. Now their wrists were tied together with a white silk ribbon. The music became extremely merry. Most people were tapping their feet to the rhythm. The two elderly ladies walked away as the music became quite wild. It seemed to set everyone there on fire. It caused Clare and Ned to go into a wild sort of dance; round and round they danced, hands held high and tied together. Clare wore an extremely pretty dress, with a red sash to match Ned's, who had on a white shirt, black trousers, and his red sash. They danced, whirled and twisted; each movement meant something to their partner, while their blood mixed on their wrists.

At last the music died to a merry tempo. Their wrists were untied by each pulling on a side of the bow knot. Clare put the ribbon in her bosom.

The fiddlers started again — such a dance as many had never seen. It seemed like the dance of their young lives. The music was so fanciful that the guests clapped and swayed with it. Like the first dance, once again each movement denoted a promise to the other partner. Ned promised to protect Clare and care for her all his life; Clare promised to minister to Ned's needs, to love honour and obey him always.

At last it was finished. Ned and Clare were married. Several Romany dancers took to the floor now, while the fiddlers went into playing fantastically beautiful, and almost hypnotic music. What a scene.

"How long does this last?" asked the vicar (tompad) of Pa' Jobey.

"It must go on until dawn" he was told.

There was plenty of food available, with many kinds of drink.

*   *   *

Meanwhile old Jimmy Williams went back to Long Barn Farm to shut in his chicken against the fox. He had almost got to the green where the farm was, when he suddenly reined in his horse. There walking across the green towards his house were the two didakais that had beat him up. This time they were accompanied by a third man.

There they were, three of the roughest types one could ever meet and heading over towards his place. He knew that he dare not go there alone. That could be fatal. He also knew they were out for revenge, thinking that the farm was empty owing to the wedding. So he turned his pony and jingle, and went back to Bunter's Farm as fast as he could.

On arrival, he called Jobey over, and told him what he had seen. Jobey stopped the dancing and merry-making by stopping the fiddlers.

Everyone at this stage of the wedding was quite high in spirit. As soon as Jobey had their attention, he explained what was going on at Long Barn Farm, the bride's home. Instantly about a dozen young men led by Madcap ran for their horses. Away they raced lickety-split over to the green. Here they split up to converge on the home of Jimmy Williams from several directions.

As they swept into the yard, they caught two men red-handed trying to smash up a partly-built vardo. The third man was spotted in the farmhouse kitchen. The riders jumped from their horses and charged straight after them. They were completely taken by surprise and tried to defend themselves as best they could — so they ran for it — only to be brought down by flying tackles, and to be really punched up for what they had done.

Ned and Tosho had run to the farmhouse to find that the man in there had smashed lots of things in the kitchen. On seeing what was happening to his mates out in the yard, through the kitchen window, he tried to run for it, only to be brought down in a flying tackle by Tosho. Ned was quickly on the scene to dish out a bit of rough justice to the man's face. He was dragged over to the barn where old Jimmy was recognizing the other two men as the same ones that had attacked him on the pretence of buying a vardo. By now they really were in a sorry state.

"You thought I was away, and that it was a good chance to get your own back on me, didn't you? Well that's where you were wrong my beauties, and we haven't finished with you yet. Right lads, I suggest we drag 'em — free of charge mind you — and only because we are good-hearted, for exactly one mile, just to let 'em know that should they live through it, never to come near here again, because if you do you will be hung from the rafters of this old barn, then dumped into the old well. Right lads, what are we waiting for?"

One man was crying at this stage, saying that he was told that Jimmy had cheated the other two men. That's why he had come along to help them.

"We cheat nobody" replied Jimmy. "You should have checked your facts."

He was still begging for mercy as a rope was passed under his arms; his hands having been tied behind his back, as were his companions'.

The riders mounted up, and off they went dragging the three didakai men behind their horses.

They gave them about a mile drag; untied the ropes, leaving them outside of the doctor's house. Out of the goodness of their hearts you understand. There they left them and rode away.

One staggered to his feet, he really was in a sorry state — his clothes were almost ripped from his body. If anyone ever had gravel rash — he did. What happened to them no one knows. But they never ever showed their faces in Tisbury again.

Ned found that the man had gained entry into the farmhouse by breaking the kitchen window. Quite a lot of Clare's crockery was smashed. Some damage was done to Jimmy's new vardo that was under construction. Paraffin oil had been splashed about, indicating that the men were going to burn the place down. However the riders had got there in time, and had saved the day.

What a good job old Jimmy had decided to pay a visit to shut up his hens for the night. Yes those three felt the rod of Romany justice.

Old Jimmy decided to stay at the farm now, with Madcap for company, who had volunteered to help clean up the mess, while the others returned to carry on with the wedding merry-making.

The dancing must go on until dawn. And so it did; the fiddlers were soon back on the job, and the dancers were dancing once more.

All this time old Ma' King sat silently smoking her old swegler (pipe) showing absolutely no emotion at all about the excitement going on around her.

Dawn came creeping in at last to give a good clear sunrise; except for a bit of mess at Long Barn all seemed to be normal.

Nobody in the area ever troubled the Romany riders again. Mainly because of the coming of the railroad, which brought more constables into the area.

And that was Romany Justice.